PAUL BROWN
THE MAN WHO INVENTED
MODERN FOOTBALL

George Cantor

TRIUMPH
BOOKS

Library of Congress Cataloging-in-Publication Data

Cantor, George, 1941-
    Paul Brown : the man who invented modern football / George Cantor.
      p. cm.
    ISBN-13: 978-1-57243-725-8
    ISBN-10: 1-57243-725-1
      1. Brown, Paul, 1908- 2. Football coaches--United States--Biography.
    I. Title.
    GV939.B77C36 2008
    796.332092--dc22
    [B]

2008003686

This book is available in quantity at special discounts for your group or organization. For further information, contact:

Triumph Books
542 South Dearborn Street
Suite 750
Chicago, Illinois 60605
(312) 939-3330
Fax (312) 663-3557

Printed in U.S.A.
ISBN: 978-1-57243-725-8
Design by Sue Knopf. Production by Amy Carter.
Photos courtesy of Getty Images, Associated Press, and Wire Images, unless otherwise noted.

Contents

Foreword

That anyone would have to be reminded of who Paul Brown was is disconcerting to me.

It's no exaggeration to say that he is the father of the modern game of football. He changed the game. His approach to coaching, the degree of organization, his dealings with his players—all of them were masterful.

He was probably the greatest teacher the game has ever seen. Really, the first teacher among professional coaches. The eight years I spent with him as an assistant coach with the Cincinnati Bengals had an impact on me that lasted the rest of my career.

Paul understood and respected the way men learned. He made sure that every one of his players knew exactly what was expected of him, not only in the plays he ran on the field, but in the other aspects of life, too. He put it all right on the table and his methods were proven by his success.

Of course, everyone wants to emulate success. So when other coaches saw the results of Paul's approach, they adopted it, too. He set the standard that is still in use today.

He knew that professional football is a serious business and he never hesitated to make the tough decisions. That is never easy. I found that out when I was a head coach. But he was as empathetic as he could be, because he knew he was affecting people's lives. I hope that I was able to borrow some of that approach, too.

To a certain degree I did use elements of Paul's thinking in devising what's come to be known as the "West Coast offense." When I worked with him, though, he wasn't that much of a hands-on technician anymore. His approach to running an offense was pretty much set. I just took away what I could from watching it being run.

But I'm still proud of what we accomplished with the Bengals in such a short time. We were in the playoffs in our third year of existence, despite losing the quarterback we'd been counting on.

That was an exhilarating experience. And, of course, the games we played against the Cleveland Browns were unforgettable. Every one of them seemed to be close, going down to the last minute or two.

Paul never had to talk to the team about how much those games meant to him. We all knew. The Browns had been his whole life. Some things don't need to be said.

He hired me in his first year in Cincinnati on the recommendation of his top assistant, Tiger Johnson. I think he liked me because I was a Stanford guy. He'd had good experience with Stanford guys and respected the school. I'm glad it worked out that way.

Our relationship grew into a very strong off the field friendship, even after I left the Bengals to coach the 49ers. We worked together on some NFL committees, and it was a bit strange that when we won our first Super Bowl, after the 1981 season, it was against Paul's Bengals. Of course, he wasn't coaching anymore and was in the front office by then.

It will happen to all of us, eventually. Once we get out of the public eye our ranking as coaches will kind of slide down. That's the way life is.

But if there is any list of great coaches that has any meaning, the name right at the top has to be Paul Brown.

—Bill Walsh

1

Down the Memory Hole

Professional football does not spend much time venerating its past. It is a game adopted and enriched by television, and like television, it thrives on images of what's happening right now. The great names and events that came before this symbiosis fade into shadow. The old images are in black and white, lacking immediacy and drama. The players don't resemble Darth Vader: there are no face guards, so you can actually see what the men look like. Everything looks smaller, too, and less important.

Some date the change, the point at which the past began to recede at the speed of light, to the 1958 NFL championship game. That is when the Baltimore Colts defeated the New York Giants in overtime of what was quickly labeled "the greatest game in history." Nothing that went before could match it, decreed the media.

This was followed by the Vince Lombardi dynasty in Green Bay, Wisconsin, and the advent of the Super Bowls. It was also during this time that professional football started marketing its games as mythic struggles, epic in significance, and fought by men with godlike personalities.

Yes, the sport does have its Hall of Fame in Canton, Ohio, but reverence for the game's past doesn't compare with baseball's dedication to ancestor worship. Babe Ruth, Ty Cobb, Cy Young, Walter Johnson—those names are magic, undimmed by time. Neither Ted Williams nor Joe DiMaggio had played a game in four decades when they died, yet many newspapers ran their obituaries on the front page. It's the same thing with managers: Connie Mack, John McGraw, Casey Stengel. Even those with only the most rudimentary knowledge of baseball know who they are.

But their peers in football, both coaches and players, are all but forgotten. When Don Hutson passed away, for example, he got a few paragraphs on most sports pages. But in the history of pro football he occupies a niche comparable to Ruth's. He was a receiver so skilled, so impossible to cover man to man, that he forced a change in standard pass defenses when he joined the Green Bay Packers in the 1930s.

Greasy Neale, Buddy Parker—only the cognoscenti recognize the names of these coaches. But both of them achieved the rare feat of repeating as NFL champions.

Incredibly, the same fate seems to be overtaking Paul Brown.

It's pretty hard to forget a man for whom a football team and two stadiums are named. But the world tries its best. In most Internet polls, for example, when voters are asked to name the greatest coaches of all time, you will usually find Lombardi listed at number one. There will also be Bill Walsh, Chuck Noll, and Don Shula. All of them were repeat Super Bowl winners, and all of them figure prominently in games aired on ESPN Classic. Their presence remains vivid.

But Lombardi made a close study of Brown's coaching techniques and applied them almost unchanged at Green Bay. Walsh, Noll, and Shula either played for or coached with Brown. Their own approaches to coaching were heavily influenced by him. Walsh, for example, is credited with devising the West Coast offense. But he freely admits that this ball-control-by-short-pass attack was originated and perfected by Brown's Cleveland teams and that he learned it as Brown's assistant in Cincinnati.

Before winning his third Super Bowl in 2005, New England coach Bill Belichick also paid homage to Brown. "So many of the things that we do today...were the same things Paul Brown did," he said. "The same schedule, the same philosophy, the same approach to getting your team to perform to the highest level on the practice field, in meetings, in strategy, in game situations. The level that he was at, I think, was way ahead of the competition at that point. And it's very, very much the blueprint for the way the game is played today."

But Brown never coached in a Super Bowl. His last championship was won in 1955, which is now part of the game's dark ages. So he seldom makes those Internet lists. Few, however, can match his résumé.

Brown created the most successful high school football program in America at Massillon Washington High School in Massillon, Ohio. At Ohio State University, he won a national championship in his second season.

While he was coaching at Great Lakes Naval Training Base during World War II, his makeshift team throttled Notre Dame. His Cleveland Browns played in 10 consecutive championship games, winning seven of them.

When he finished his career with the Cincinnati Bengals, he had them in the playoffs in their third season, a record for an expansion team at the time.

The list of his innovations is incredible. He was the first coach to:

- call plays for his quarterback

- give his players IQ and personality tests

- hire an all-year staff of assistant coaches

- scout opponents through game films

- require his players to pass written exams on the material in their playbooks

- keep the entire team together in a hotel the night before a home game

- hold practices in which every drill was organized in advance

- systematize the college draft

- design a passing offense that attacked specific areas of an opponent's defense, and then devise defenses to counter the offense he had created

And if the firsts weren't enough, he also:

- devised the first face guard for helmets

- invented the taxi squad

- shattered the color barrier in pro football

- invented the draw play

It is, in fact, no exaggeration when Belichick says that Brown invented modern football. Even George Halas, a founder of the NFL and one of its seminal coaching figures, credited Brown with turning the league into an organized, highly skilled endeavor instead of a bunch of big lugs whaling the daylights out of each other.

Brown's overall coaching record was 347–135–15. If you throw out his last eight years with an expansion franchise, his winning percentage was .783. His teams were so dominant that on two occasions rivals told him they simply could not compete.

All but four of those 41 seasons were spent within the state of Ohio. Brown came to believe that growing up with solid Midwestern values, of which Ohio was the exemplar, molded the players he preferred. He took special care to fill his rosters with them.

He was a rather austere man. Chilly, some would say. *The New York Times* once described him as "the cold, calculating genius of the lakefront." He could be, by turns, a visionary or an ogre.

Tommy James, a halfback who played for him at Massillon, Ohio State, and with the Browns, put it this way, "I wouldn't say I loved him. I respected him. Just like anybody who's got you under his thumb. You bitch. Cuss him out under your breath...I could be wrong. Thought a lot of him, the players. I would never use the word *love*. Like, yes."

Most of his players felt that way. But many feared him, and only a few recall him with affection. That also contributes to his diminished memory.

To his friends outside the game, he could be a delightful companion: well-read, a talented piano player, an avid golfer and card player, a wry wit. But he firmly believed that a head coach had no friends on his team.

"We are all useful, but no one is necessary." He adopted that motto as his own at the very beginning in Massillon, and it served him for the rest of his career.

That career spanned the start of the Great Depression to the end of the Vietnam War. At its conclusion, he found himself living in a time when his methods no longer worked. America had changed too much. The attitudes of the past had become part of a foreign place, even in his beloved Ohio. In a culture that regards 15 years ago as "back in the day," it all slides down the memory hole. In getting at the reasons behind Brown's mastery it is useful to examine the most critical games of his coaching career. Many of them were chosen by Brown himself in an interview late in his life. The additional choices suggest other aspects of his career. If you were to select 10 such games, they would be these:

1. 1935: Massillon Washington High School vs. Canton McKinley High School

2. 1940: Massillon Washington High School vs. Toledo Waite High School

3. 1941: Ohio State University vs. University of Michigan

4. 1942: Ohio State University vs. University of Michigan

5. 1946: Cleveland Browns vs. New York Yankees

6. 1950: Cleveland Browns vs. Philadelphia Eagles

7. 1950: Cleveland Browns vs. Los Angeles Rams

8. 1954: Cleveland Browns vs. Detroit Lions

9. 1955: Cleveland Browns vs. Los Angeles Rams

10. 1970: Cincinnati Bengals vs. Cleveland Browns

The stories of those games are the stories of the man.

But to really understand, you must go back to Massillon, the battered old steel town in the heart of Ohio.

2

Carry On for Massillon

Lester Brown was a railroad man, a dispatcher. His job was to make sure the trains ran on time.

He would assign a daily task for his son, Paul, leave it written on a slate in the kitchen, and reward him with a few pennies when it was done to his satisfaction. Brown learned the lesson well: diligence and meticulous preparation pay off.

Kenny Anderson, his last great quarterback, said, tellingly, that playing on a Paul Brown team was like riding on an express train.

"There was a certitude of being on a train that hit every station exactly on time," he said. "Somehow when the process ended the train would come to a smooth stop. That's the feeling he passed on to his quarterback, and it helped in your preparation."

Brown's mother, Ida, was a card player and highly competitive. She would wait for young Paul to finish his schoolwork and then instruct him on the finer points of getting an edge on your opponent at rummy and other games. Brown learned that lesson, too: pay attention to every detail of what your opponent is doing.

"He sent 11 scouts to every game McKinley High played," said Ick Martin, captain of his 1939 team at Massillon. "If you had the right tackle, you wrote down every movement that he made. Now that's detail. One man on each guy—and you better have on your report what he did on each play."

"Nothing escaped his attention," says Junie Studer, a longtime Massillon football booster and team historian. "The captain of his 1935 team was Augie Morningstar. He had been the starting center for two years. Before the season began Brown said he wanted him to play end. Augie couldn't understand it. 'I've been watching you for three years,' Brown told him. 'At the end of every play they toss the ball to the center. You've never dropped one. You're my end.'"

But the skills Brown brought to his later work all may have gone for naught if it hadn't been for a move and Massillon's football mania. The railroad transferred the Brown family from his birthplace in Norwalk, Ohio, to Massillon, Ohio, in 1917. Brown was nine years old.

Norwalk is a gracious town in the state's Western Reserve, with an appearance and texture that reflect its traditional New England roots. It was an idyllic place to grow up in the early years of the 20th century.

But in Massillon, football was everything. That arbitrary corporate relocation led Brown to his destiny.

"Here was a steel-mill town," says Mike Brown, president of the Cincinnati Bengals and the coach's son. "But when I was growing up there I thought it was a beautiful town. The people who were from Massillon all thought so, too."

Football transformed the place and made it magical. From a dingy outpost of Republic Steel Corporation it became Tigertown; where orange-and-black banners waved from every downtown lamppost to lift the hearts of its residents, and a caravan of cars paraded merrily to the stadium on autumn Friday evenings to cheer the Tigers on.

A former mayor called it "a rallying point for the community, through the bad times economically and the good times."

The city's legendary sportswriter, Luther Emery, of the Massillon *Independent*, once wrote that "football is bred in Massillonians. The native citizen has heard it talked about from the time he opens his eyes in the cradle."

Chris Spielman, who went on to All American and Pro Bowl honors at Ohio State University and then to the Detroit Lions, says that "I played for them. I played for the town, consciously."

A huge wall mural at the town's main downtown intersection carries a tribute composed by Iowa sportswriter Ron Maly in 1978:

> In the beginning, when the Great Creator was drawing plans for this world of ours, He decided there should be something for everyone. He gave us mountains that reach to the sky, deep blue seas, green forests, dry deserts, gorgeous flowers, and gigantic trees. Then He decided there should be football, and He gave us Massillon. He created only one Massillon; He knew that would be enough.

On the left side of the mural is a portrait of Brown. On the bottom is the motto: Win or Lose, Massillon Always.

The name Massillon is French, but not because the French were the first settlers. It was actually founded in 1826 as an American canal town along the Tuscarawas River and grew quickly as a shipping point for grain from local farms up to the lake port of Cleveland. But the wife of its founder was a great admirer of the writing of the French clergyman Jean-Baptiste Massillon, and she was given naming honors.

Within seven years, the town's main product had shifted to iron, and the discovery of coal deposits nearby enhanced its industrial muscle. And Massillon is where Coxey's Army of the unemployed began its celebrated march on Washington, D.C. during an economic depression in 1894. But there was a solid core of prosperity in Massillon. The great stone mansions that still line Fourth Street, east of downtown, attest to the wealth that flowed into the area.

When Brown was growing up the main road was U.S. 30, the Lincoln Highway. It was the first great transcontinental auto route, carrying travelers off to the greater world. A Massillon downtown street is still called Lincoln Way, although Highway 30 now bypasses the center of town.

In those years, Massillon's population was around 26,000, only a bit smaller than it is today.

Massillon named its high school Washington, after the U.S. president. Canton, the bigger, richer, and more politically wired city to the east of Massillon and also in Stark County, has a high school named William McKinley High, which was named for its very own hometown president.

When Brown moved to Massillon, the neighboring city was four times as large, the eighth in size in Ohio. Yet the competition between the two places was even and fierce, especially on the gridiron.

High school football in Massillon can be traced back to 1894, although official recognition didn't come until 10 years later. By 1909, according to Massillon Washington High School's athletics department history, it was awarding letters and had claimed the championship of northeastern Ohio by twice defeating Canton Central High School.

That was no small claim. In this part of the state, football had taken hold as a semireligious preoccupation. The game already was well established nationally. College teams from the Ivy League, the University of Michigan, and the University of Chicago had won national titles. The first Rose Bowl had been played, with the point-a-minute Michigan team trampling Stanford University, 49–0. But the roots of the professional game were being planted in Ohio, in Akron, Canton, and Massillon, by amateur teams.

The first team to be called the Massillon Tigers was organized in 1903 as a member of a loose-jointed amateur association called the Ohio League. According to historians Bob Braunwart and Bob Carroll of the Professional Football Researchers Association, the Tigers quickly violated league rules by paying four players imported from Pittsburgh in the season's final game against Akron. Massillon won 12–0 and then divvied up the profits among the entire team, thereby turning them all into professional players. The Tigers were vilified in the press, but in 1905, their opponents began paying their players, too.

In that same year, and perhaps just as significant, Canton entered its own team in the league and called it the Bulldogs. It didn't take long for bad blood to flow. The new Canton team scheduled a game with the Carlisle Indian Industrial School of Pennsylvania, and then stipulated that Carlisle could not play another game in Stark County that year. The thought was that Massillon would then be frozen out of a potentially big gate amount.

But Massillon went ahead, signed a contract with Carlisle, and simply transferred the game to Cleveland. It was a financial success, and by the time the Ohio teams played each other in the final game of the season, a suitably nasty tone had been set.

The Tigers won, finishing a perfect 10-0 season and winning their third straight Ohio League title. Victory bonfires burned through the night, and brass bands paraded downtown.

Canton would not stand for this. After all, it was the bigger and richer city. So in 1906 it began hiring all the college stars it could find who were willing to come down to Ohio to help bash Massillon. The Tigers retaliated and spent freely to bring in their own athletes.

In a cycle that is all too familiar to contemporary sports fans, both teams managed to spend themselves into insolvency. Massillon, nonetheless, won its fourth straight title (although Canton did snap its three-year winning streak). Then the Massillon manager, who was also a journalist, accused the Bulldogs in print of throwing the final game to hype a profitable third meeting between the teams.

The charge was never proven, but it killed Canton at the gate. The team folded, and with the competition thus weakened, Massillon stopped importing big names. It fielded a team of local talent instead and still won the championship again in 1907. But the rivalry between the two cities had turned into a deep hatred. They would not play each other again for eight years.

During the first five seasons of the Ohio League, Massillon ran up a record of 42-2-1. It was so dominant that it killed off interest in the sport in other towns, a phenomenon that also arose during Brown's career there.

By 1915, however, a resuscitated Canton team once again decided to go after major stars. It settled on the biggest of them all, Jim Thorpe. With this internationally famous athlete—some would say the greatest player ever—in their backfield, the Bulldogs won three titles in the next four years.

Massillon felt the need to retaliate. It signed the two biggest names at Notre Dame, Knute Rockne and Gus Dorais. Even with them, however, the Tigers weren't quite good enough to match Canton. But the spending wars had once more taken the two teams to the edge of bankruptcy.

Professional teams from all around the country, in fact, were coming to realize that they couldn't continue without a formal structure and some spending controls. It was this situation that prompted a 1920 meeting of team owners in a downtown Canton car dealership. It resulted in formation of the American Professional Football Association—the direct antecedent of the National Football League.

This meeting is why Canton claims to be the birthplace of the league and why the NFL located its Hall of Fame there. It was a decision strongly supported by Brown.

Both Canton and Massillon had teams in the new league. All the league's teams were, in fact, based in smaller towns. But the need to get a foothold in major markets soon resulted in franchise shifts to New York, Chicago, Philadelphia, and Pittsburgh. With the exception of the Green Bay Packers, all the original teams disappeared long ago, including the Massillon Tigers and the Canton Bulldogs.

But in this corner of Ohio, football fever raged unabated. If the Tigers and Bulldogs would no longer clash as professional teams, then the largest high schools in the two cities would carry on the old grudge under the same names.

Massillon did not join the state's High School Athletic Association until 1916, but its games with Canton go back to the beginning of its football history, 22 years prior. The early games did not go so well. Canton won 13 of the first 14 meetings between the schools, with one ending in a scoreless tie. On 11 occasions, Massillon failed to score a point.

But in 1909, the balance started to shift, and Massillon won six of the next nine games. The series was not played every year, and in 1918 the game had to be canceled because of the Spanish flu epidemic. It would have been Massillon's first game against Canton McKinley High School, which opened that fall in a new building to replace the aging Central High.

That initial meeting between Massillon and its old enemy with the new name was delayed until 1919. Massillon won 21–0, and the great rivalry was on. Thirty-four times the winner of this game would be Ohio state champions. By the time Brown entered Massillon Washington in 1922, the tradition of playing McKinley in the season finale, the weekend after Thanksgiving, was established.

But long before high school, football was very much a part of Brown's life. He recalled playing football even back in Norwalk as a child. "When the bladder went," he wrote later, "we stuffed it with leaves and feathers and went on playing."

When he entered high school in Massillon, though, he immersed himself in his studies and decided that the pole vault would be his athletic outlet. He weighed less than 150 pounds. Even in the early 1920s that was small for a football player.

Massillon had a different outlook on these things, though. Just before Brown arrived, the team had been quarterbacked by Harry Stuhldreher, who was just about the same size. Stuhldreher went on to play for Notre Dame and became one of the famed Four Horsemen, backs noted for their quickness rather than size.

Coach Dave Stewart was a great believer in speed as the factor that could equalize all things. Stewart had led Massillon to its first state title in 1922, when Brown was a freshman. Stewart's team outscored its opponents 379–34 in a 10–0 season, including a 24–0 whipping of McKinley.

Stewart was also the track coach. Regarding Brown, the coach was at first amused and then impressed by the undersized and unskilled young man's determination to be a vaulter. But he thought that competitive quality could be transferred to other endeavors. In 1924 Brown took over as Stewart's starting quarterback as a junior.

"I was so obsessed with it, I don't think I knew my own limitations," Brown said later.

Before the season began, Stewart took his young quarterback to Cedar Point, Ohio, to get away from everything and to talk about football. It was a favorite getaway for Rockne, Notre Dame's fabled head coach, too. Rockne had perfected the forward pass while working as a lifeguard with Dorais on the Lake Erie beach. The two would later spring the play on an unsuspecting Army team in an historic upset. Rockne even went back there with Stuhldreher to talk things over before that Massillon player took over as Notre Dame's starting quarterback. So the precedent was established.

Stewart said later of Brown that something in the young man's enthusiasm and eagerness to learn won his confidence. He was also fast, the way Stewart liked his players. And he knew how to take charge. "When he called signals," Stewart said, "his voice rang out like Napoleon."

"David—he was my everything," Brown said in later life.

Brown repaid his mentor with a record of 15-3 in his two seasons as a starter. In his senior year, however, when he also captained the Tigers, his final game at Massillon ended in a 6-3 defeat to Canton. It was only the second time McKinley had beaten Massillon, and it stung.

On Stewart's recommendation, Brown enrolled at Ohio State in the fall of 1926. He hoped to live the dream of every red-blooded Ohioan and make the Buckeye squad. But for once in his life Brown was overreaching.

Ohio State was loaded with talent and had a team that challenged for the Big Ten title. In front of a record Ohio Stadium crowd of 90,000, however, the Bucks lost the big one to the University of Michigan 17–16. Ohio battled back from a touchdown behind in the fourth quarter, only to watch a missed extra point decide it.

What made the pill all the tougher to swallow was that the loss came in the midst of six consecutive losses to the Wolverines. This was not yet the greatest rivalry in college sports, not yet played on the final Saturday of the season, but it was still a date that both schools marked on their calendars.

Fifteen years later, one of Brown's most memorable games as a coach would follow an almost identical scenario. But in 1926 he was only a spectator. When he showed up to try out for the team, he wasn't even given a uniform. Skinny little quarterbacks might cut it in high school, but not in the Big Ten.

When that dream died, though, Brown fashioned another. After his freshman year, he transferred to Miami University, in Oxford, Ohio. It may have been a step down in competitive grade, but not in tradition. In years to come, this school would be famous as the "cradle of coaches." An astonishing number of Hall of Fame inductees were associated with Miami, either as players or coaches.

Brown was not the first. The line goes all the way back to Red Blaik, class of 1918, who guided two Army teams to national championships and was, in turn, the mentor to Vince Lombardi.

Preceding Brown as Miami's quarterback was Weeb Ewbank. He later became one of Brown's top assistants in Cleveland and remains the only man ever to win a pro football championship with two different franchises—the Baltimore Colts of 1958 and 1959 and the New York Jets of 1968.

Sid Gillman, Woody Hayes, Ara Parseghian, Bo Schembechler, John Pont—all of them and more would come through Miami.

But when Brown joined the football team in 1927, this was still in the future. The coach was Chester Pittser, who wasn't in anyone's cradle. He doubled as baseball coach and was far more successful on the diamond. Miami won three Buckeye Conference titles under his guidance. But in football he was only 41-25-2 over eight seasons. Nonetheless, Pittser's best run of success came with Brown running his team. For those two seasons he was 14-3.

Brown's years at Miami also gave him further insight into preparing for huge, season-defining games. He had played in Massillon-Canton and watched Ohio State-Michigan. In this case, it was Miami-Cincinnati.

The teams first met in 1888, the first college football game ever played in Ohio. They also claim it is the oldest football series west of the Alleghenies. (It isn't quite continuous, though. They have played each other 112 times over 120 years.)

In Brown's seasons as a starter, the Big Red won twice, by scores of 34-0 and 14-6. In the second game, he went all the way on a badly sprained ankle.

Brown had beaten Cincinnati on one good leg. He expected no less from his players. In years to come, he would show little patience with players who used injuries as an excuse for what he regarded as a lackluster performance. "Maybe," Brown would tell them with a stare that penetrated the core of their being, "you're just not good enough."

The players to whom those words were directed still remember it as one of the most devastating moments of their lives.

Brown's field of study had been prelaw, but the idea of going on for that degree did not appeal to him. He was keenly interested in history and read widely in the field. There were indications that he might be in line for a Rhodes Scholarship.

But this was 1930, and the Great Depression was settling in hard. A job anywhere would be a treasure worth keeping.

Before his senior season at Miami he had gone to Sharon, Pennsylvania, to assist Stewart, his old coach, who had taken over the high school team there. The two had remained close friends. Early the following year Stewart heard about a job opening at an elite Maryland preparatory school, Severn School.

Severn had hired one of the finest athletes in the state's history to coach its football team. Fred Linkous won nine letters in football, basketball, and lacrosse at the University of Maryland. This job was seen as the first step in what assuredly would be a brilliant coaching career.

But Linkous contracted a throat infection that could not be healed. It turned out to be cancer. He died in March 1930 at the age of 24.

Brown had a much less inspiring resume and was not quite 22 years old. But time was short, and Stewart's judgment was trusted. On his say-so, Brown got the job for the 1930 football season.

Severn had been founded in 1914. Its mission was to mold the character and intellect that would create suitable candidates for the U.S. Naval Academy in nearby Annapolis. Brown felt at home in a setting that combined academic excellence with a rigorous semimilitary discipline. That's what he wanted in his football players, too.

It seemed to the young coach that one of the Severn players in particular had the right sort of Ohio values, despite hailing from Illinois. Brown recalled later that the right guard on his first Severn team, Slade Cutter, would enter the Naval Academy and go on to beat favored Army with a last-minute field goal. He would also be elected to the College Football Hall of Fame. More important, as a submarine captain in World War II, he was awarded the Navy Cross four times and was credited with sinking more Japanese ships than any other patrol group in the Pacific war.

Brown's success at Severn was prompt and decisive. In two seasons his teams went 12-2-1. According to Brown's figures, written much later in life, his teams went 16-1-1. But the school yearbook's game-by-game account of these two seasons gives a different total. The *Anchor and Wheel* also describes Brown as having attended Kiskiminetas Prep School in Pennsylvania for a year. That credit appears in no other summary of his life. There is a strong possibility that he had to offer some sort of preppy background in order to get this job.

In Brown's first season, Severn won its second consecutive Maryland state championship, sweeping through a seven-game schedule undefeated. With only one returning starter, the team went a highly creditable 5-2-1 in 1931.

At Severn, however, football was just a sport, one among many. The school felt that it taught some useful lessons to a young man. (A quote from the *Anchor and Wheel* yearbook reads: "If properly directed...it can create in him an enthusiasm which will become a spur to greater effort in his studies.") Therefore, it was mildly encouraged as one learning experience out of many.

The all-encompassing love for football shared by those in Massillon was missing at Severn for Brown. It wasn't the same at all. The young coach understood that if he were to rise in the profession that seemed to have been thrust upon him, he would have to go to a community that shared his unstinting dedication to the sport.

Then the unbelievable occurred. The Massillon job, the position he didn't even dare to dream about, became available. And the man the school wanted was Brown.

3

1935: Massillon Washington 6, Canton McKinley 0

Paul Brown often said the only two jobs he had ever wanted were the head coach positions at Massillon Washington High School and at Ohio State University.

"Paul loved Massillon," said his sister, Marian Evans. "It meant everything to him."

"He would say the happiest times of his life were when he was a coach at Massillon," said his son, Mike Brown. "It was where he felt he did the most good. He had no vision beyond going to Massillon, which to him was the grandest thing possible. That was his home. That was where football was important. He knew the people. He knew the environment."

In later life, when Brown was nationally known, he would always find time to do favors for friends from the old days in Massillon, Ohio. After leaving for Ohio State in 1941 he never lived there again. But he always regarded it as home, and it was there that he asked to be buried.

When he returned in 1932, however, Massillon was a bit puzzled. Everyone knew his name, of course, but the idea that this 24-year-old kid, barely two years out of college, could restore Tigers football to the pinnacle it had occupied under Stewart seemed absurd.

Stewart departed for Sharon, Ohio, the same year Brown graduated from high school. In the intervening six seasons, Massillon was barely a .500 team. In 1931 the Tigers hit bottom, winning just two of 10 games. They had been battered by Toledo's Scott High School,

27-0, and by Steubenville High School, 68-0. No one in recent memory had run up scores like that on Massillon: that was what Massillon did to other cities. Even a 20-6 win over Canton McKinley High School couldn't salvage the season for Coach Elmer McGrew. He was dismissed by popular demand, and a search for a replacement began.

School board president H.W. Bell had kept in touch with Brown's old coach Dave Stewart and asked for input on a list put together by the search committee. Stewart unequivocally recommended Brown for his intensity, obsessive dedication to organization and detail, and self-assurance that would not admit to doubt. All of it had registered with Stewart.

Bell interviewed Brown and expressed the reservation that he would repeat frequently during Brown's tenure at Massillon. Bell felt that the young man may have been "wound a little too tight" for a job like this. Because, said Bell, "the hammers" were always just below the surface in this town. In the end, though, the force of his intellect and clear love of Massillon carried the day. He was given the job.

Brown arrived to find a program that was not only diminished on the field but in its psyche as well. The school board was broke in this most terrible of Great Depression years. All the team's equipment was retreads, even down to the shoes. Some of the players were going hungry at dinnertime. A sense of hopelessness prevailed, as it did in much of the country. So the first order of business was to restore Massillon's pride.

A published recollection by local sportswriter Luther Emery details Brown's approach to his new job. According to Emery, Brown made a point of studying the methods of other coaches. He said later he learned just as much from the bad ones as from the good ones because he discovered what not to do. He fired an assistant coach almost immediately for showing up late to practice because he was working his farm.

No excuses would be tolerated. None.

Having come from the semimilitary environment at Severn School, Brown was an admirer of Chick Meehan, the coach at New York University. Meehan had turned NYU into a national power in the 1920s, playing before crowds of 50,000 and more at Yankee Stadium.

His teams were noted for their military precision. All the linemen would take their positions in unison, arms and bodies swinging in tight coordination, as if conducting a drill. To heighten the impression, Meehan had a cannon fired after each New York touchdown. According to school legend, his star running back, Ken Strong, scored so often one afternoon that the cannon ran out of ammunition. Meehan even made his players jump rope when they came off the field.

This sort of discipline seemed exactly right to Brown, a way to build *esprit de corps* for a team whose *esprit* was a corpse. What worked with college players, however, didn't quite make it with high schoolers playing in someone else's shoes. Emery wrote that Brown gave up on most of those ideas midway through his first season. But he retained other Meehan rules: there would be no water buckets on the sidelines, and every player would stand when he was not in the game. No one was allowed to sit on the bench. That's not how Tigers were made.

On a more practical level, Brown said that he was heavily influenced by the offensive scheme of Duke University's coach, Jimmy DeHart. Brown had studied DeHart's offense while at Severn, even attending a coaching clinic in order to learn it. DeHart employed a double-wingback formation, which used speed and deception as its chief weapons. When Duke defeated a heavily favored Navy team in 1930, it suddenly became football's new big thing. More important, DeHart's philosophy coincided with Brown's own approach to the game, one he had learned from Stewart: speed rather than strength was the one irreplaceable ingredient.

Brown also studied the line-blocking theories of Purdue University head coach Noble Kizer. An almost forgotten name now, Kizer had been one of the Seven Mules as a guard on Notre Dame's Four Horsemen teams. He turned Purdue into a national power in the early 1930s and still has the best winning percentage of any Boilermakers coach. His reputation was so good that in a national vote of fans he was selected to coach the college team in football's first All-Star Game in 1934. And as with DeHart, it was Kizer's emphasis on quickness in his linemen with sudden shifts in blocking assignments that appealed to Brown. It was a concept transmitted directly from the agile mind of coaching legend Knute Rockne.

Brown's methods worked for almost exactly half a season. His Tigers swept through their first five games, pummeling two teams from Akron. But thin talent and a lack of depth caught up with them. After a scoreless tie with Barberton High School, Massillon's Tigers dropped their last four in a row, getting shut out in three of them. That included a 19-0 drubbing by McKinley.

Still, a 5-4-1 year was an improvement. Massillon was willing to give some space to the young coach, understanding that he had some work to do. The town would have been a lot cheerier had it realized that those four season-ending losses represented exactly half the games the Tigers would lose during Brown's entire nine-year tenure at Massillon.

Brown saw football as only part of his assignment. The ultimate goal was to make Massillon the best in everything.

"He changed the school," says one of the team's historians, Phil Glick. "He changed the attitude in the band, in studies, in choir, and speech and debate. He had a terrific impact."

Brown organized the first booster club in Massillon and the junior high football program. He brought in a musical director, George Bird, who transformed the Massillon marching band into one of the top half-time attractions in the country. Inspired by the panther mascot of the University of Pittsburgh, Brown dreamed up Obie, the sideline symbol of the Massillon Tigers. Years before anyone else, Brown understood that football had to be part of a total experience. The music, the excitement, the pageantry, the emotional support of the community—it all went into what a successful program should be.

"Paul Brown was a firm believer that when you went to a football game, you went to be entertained," said Shirley Bird, the daughter of the band director and one of its first majorettes, quoted in Scott H. Shook's book *Massillon Memories*. "That was it. It was part of a total entertainment package."

That seems only too obvious today, when bands and tailgating are regarded as an essential part of the football experience. But Brown understood that at least 30 years before everyone else caught on.

Massillon's superintendent of schools, L.J. Smith, actually hired Bird, who had been a student of his in Fayette, Ohio. But it was Brown who urged him to put together a marching band that "could put on a good show." It was also Brown who suggested the band adopt the old Dixieland tune "Tiger Rag" as its theme.

"I never got so sick of a song in my life," said Bird. "But the people loved it."

Team historian and booster Junie Studer recalled the time Massillon went on the road and battered Mansfield High School, 33–7. Some of the Tiger boosters stayed over to celebrate.

"PB [Brown] really wanted that game because Mansfield had tied him at home the previous year," said Studer. "Well, it was a rout, and the Mansfield people weren't any too happy.

"One of my cousins, Ownie Carver, had gone to the game with some friends. Ownie ran a cigar store downtown. Massillon had the most cigar stores per capita in the country back then, so you'd think there was an awful lot of heavy smokers here. But I guess 'cigar store' was what you might call a euphemism. What they really did was take sports bets, scalp tickets, even put out some mortgages during the Depression.

"Well, Ownie liked to show off a little, and during the party he told one of his pals to ask the piano player in the bar to play 'Tiger Rag.' The piano player flat-out refused. 'You're not going to come up here and beat up on our team and then rub it in with that song,' he said.

"Same thing happened when another of Ownie's pals made the request. So Ownie says, 'I'll bet you $5 apiece I can get him to play that song.' There were about 10 of 'em at the table, and they all took him up on it.

"Ownie walks up to the guy, palms him two $20 bills, and before he could get back to the table, the piano player was into 'Hold That Tiger.' He finishes 10 bucks ahead.

"I love to tell that story because it says so much about the way Massillon was back then."

In Studer's mind, though, Massillon football didn't really grab hold of the community until Brown organized the Booster Club in 1934.

"He did it to make sure his players were going to be fed right," he says. "Those were real hard times here, and a lot of families didn't have enough to eat. He found out that one of his boys had eaten nothing but potatoes all week, and the family was boiling the skins to make soup.

"There was also the fact that if one of these farm boys stayed late and missed the bus, he had to walk home. You drive between Massillon and Canton today, and it's all built up. But back then those were farms, and lots of our best players came from them. So PB made sure they'd all get a good meal at the YMCA and a ride home after practice with a Booster Club member."

But Brown had a bit of self-interest in mind, too. He would speak at the club meetings, let the members know what was going on with the team, even diagram some plays for them. The boosters felt that they were part of it all and had a coach who was giving them a look inside. But it wasn't much of a look. Brown didn't believe in giving out a lot of information. It was just enough to keep Massillon squarely on his side.

Besides, the talent was starting to come around. Augie Morningstar and Cloyd Snavely were first-team All-State players anchoring the line. Edgar Herring was a running back so swift he was nicknamed "Echo," because that's all he left behind for an opponent. Fullback Bob Glass made the All-State team three years in a row.

Just as important, Brown was able to develop his first quarterback, Mike Byelene. The coach may have identified with him. He was also an undersized athlete who depended on quickness and stamina to get by.

"He didn't flower any speeches," Byelene said later of his coach. "He just came to exact words. He knew certain words, whether it was cutting, complimentary, to make you work harder or that he means business."

But Brown also observed the effect of his words. He spoke to Byelene harshly just one time, and when he saw the quarterback was deeply hurt he never did it again. "He just went around biting his lip," Byelene said.

Byelene was an All-State selection. But when Harry Stuhldreher, who was then head coach at the University of Wisconsin, came on a recruiting visit, he turned him down as being too small. Byelene pointed out that he was about the same size Stuhldreher was when Stuhldreher quarterbacked Massillon and went on to honors at Notre Dame. The coach was unmoved.

Brown eventually arranged for Byelene to go to Purdue, where he delighted in defeating Wisconsin the first time he played Stuhldreher's team. Brown's son, Mike, was named after him.

Brown asked a lot of his players, and on some points he was immovable. Everyone came to practices on time, preferably early, and everyone went to class. Missing either would call the furies down on a player because Brown held his assistant coaches responsible for making sure these rules were enforced.

No excuses would be tolerated. None.

In his second season at Massillon it started to come together. The Tigers lost to Barberton, 6-0, but rolled over everyone else on their schedule. Coming into the McKinley game, they were 8-1. Once again, though, the Bulldogs stuffed them, 21-0. There were low murmurs down at the "cigar stores."

Most historians point to the following season, 1934, as the year that the series with McKinley boiled over. Both teams came into this game undefeated. The winner would surely be the state champion. Massillon had won the title once, under Stewart, in 1922. McKinley had done it twice, in 1920 and in 1927. There could be no bigger game in Ohio.

Not only was Massillon unbeaten, it had not given up a point. Brown had defeated his mentor Stewart in a game against Sharon High School, 27-0. The Tigers had rolled over Cleveland's Shaw High School, 46-0; Barberton, which had beaten them the previous year, went down 54-0. Against Alliance High School the score was 65-0, and the Tigers beat Niles's McKinley High School 72-0.

The game was at Massillon, and the stadium couldn't begin to accommodate ticket demand. Temporary bleachers were erected in one end zone. It was the biggest crowd in school history.

And Massillon lost, 21-6.

The town was rocked to its soul. Not only was the perfect season in ruins, but it came at the hands of Canton McKinley, which was now the state champion. The Canton school had an enrollment almost four times bigger than Massillon's 800 students. Its players always seemed to be bigger, too.

But no excuses would be tolerated. None.

Few Massillonians could remember a day as bleak as this. For the first time, there were rumblings that Brown couldn't win the big one. Yes, his record had improved every year, and up until that final game this had been the greatest team Massillon ever had fielded. But in his three games against McKinley, he had lost every time and by a cumulative score of 61-6. Even the reviled Coach McGrew, for all his failings, had managed to beat Canton in his last three years.

According to legend, some of the influential boosters agreed among themselves that if Brown couldn't knock off Canton McKinley next time, maybe it was time for him to go. Brown's son says that he has heard the story but was never able to verify it.

"He [Paul] never mentioned it to me."

But not many things escaped Paul Brown in Massillon. If the word was out, he surely would have known it.

His 1935 team began with a roar and never let up. It was a virtual repeat of the previous season. Akron East, 70-0. Cleveland Shaw, 66-0. The closest anyone came to the Tigers was Alliance, and they lost 27-0. There was one small difference this time. Massillon actually had given up two touchdowns coming into the Canton game.

Still, apprehension ran high. Emery watched Massillon batter Niles's McKinley the previous week and thought there was reason for concern.

"What was alarming," he wrote, "was the manner in which Niles scored and the many passes they completed against the Massillon 11."

He did acknowledge, however, that most of these passes were completed against the second team. And oh, yes, the final score was 53-6.

Still, this was the Canton game. Even though the Bulldogs had been beaten twice and tied once, there were suspicions that their coach, Jimmy Aiken, was holding back something special for Massillon.

But Brown uncharacteristically acknowledged that his team should be considered the favorites.

"We expect to win," he said during the week. "This is the first time in the four years my teams have played Canton that I have said that. I think we have the better team.... The kids are ready and eager to go."

Brown never explained his reason for building up such expectations. He was fully aware of the effect his words would have on Canton. But he also knew the danger of a defeatist mentality, and he suspected that it had taken hold of his team.

Massillonians spoke openly of a jinx. Brown's four senior starters had never beaten McKinley. There were those who were convinced that Aiken had Brown's number. Brown was not about to permit this attitude to take hold.

"As Martin Luther threw his inkwell at the Devil," editorialized the *Independent*, "so if the trophy comes to Massillon we throw our inkwell at the fleeing jinx."

The sports section ran mug shots of the entire team under a headline that ran two lines deep across the top of the page: "Battle Cry of Washington High's Tigers as They Bid for Victory over Bulldogs to Give Massillon Undefeated Season on Gridiron."

The Thanksgiving season is never a balmy time of year in northeastern Ohio. But 1935 was rougher than most. It snowed the day before the game, and a bitter north wind seemed to be howling right out of Canada.

Brown took his whole team to a movie on Friday night, a practice that would become standard for him. Then they took the bus to Canton over the snow-slick Lincoln Highway on Saturday morning for the biggest game of his career.

Those who saw it say it may have been the most intense of the entire series. McKinley never substituted, and Brown sent in just three subs late in the game, and only after getting a lead. Players on both sides could barely walk off the field at the end. The most exhausted crawled on their hands and knees.

Despite Emery's misgivings, Canton completed just one pass, despite outgaining Massillon on the ground and winning the battle of first downs, 12–8.

But in the only statistic that matters, it was Glass, the All-State fullback who would go on to play at Tulane, who crashed into the end zone from fourth and two in the third quarter. And it was Brown who sprang the game-turning surprise.

McKinley blocked a punt on the Massillon 25-yard line with seconds left in the third quarter. On its lone pass completion of the game the Bulldogs moved the ball to the 6.

As the painful shadow of inevitability fell across the Massillon grandstand, Brown quickly shifted his defense into an eight-man line. He had scouted the Canton offense well and felt that it could not adjust against this alignment.

Brown had tried it out in the New Philadelphia High School game two weeks prior, the result of which was a 65–0 romp. Even the Massillon fans had jeered in that game when the coach took out his second team, put the regulars back in, and lined them up eight across in a game that was well in hand. But Brown wanted to see how his players would react in an actual game and whether any tinkering needed to be done.

The incident was forgotten—until his defense lined up against Canton as the fourth quarter began. McKinley couldn't gain a yard against the eight-man wall from the 6-yard line. Three runs were stacked up for a one-yard loss, and a fourth-down pass was swatted away.

In one of its rare, sustained drives on this day, Massillon then moved the ball out of danger and punted. McKinley never threatened again.

"The finest exhibition of football ever witnessed in Stark County, if not the whole state," cheered the *Independent*. "How those young Tigers stood fast in the trenches! Rarely are such courage and determination seen. Congratulations to the board of education for supporting the highest type of athletics and to Coach Brown for masterful training."

"Long May the Tiger Rule" read the front-page headline.

But they didn't know the half of it.

4

1940: Massillon Washington 28, Toledo Waite 0

By the end of the 1935 season, most of the methods that came to be associated with Brown's long coaching career were already in place. Organization and control were foremost.

He had systematized Massillon's junior high school football program so that a steady stream of talent would always be flowing to him. Promising players were clearly identified by the eighth grade. By the ninth grade their talents were being directed to fill the upcoming position needs on the varsity. This is a commonplace practice now, especially in successful basketball programs, but it was not in the 1930s.

Brown always denied that he was taking the fun out of the game by shaping these players at such an early age. Still, he always seemed to find time to stop by and watch the junior high practices. The players knew that the winnowing-out process had begun when they looked up and saw the man in the sweatshirt and white pants observing their every move.

The system ran so smoothly that it was almost impossible for someone who had started school outside Massillon to win a place on the team. Nonetheless, it was widely rumored that Brown conspired with Republic Steel Corporation to get the fathers of promising football players transferred to Massillon. Such tactics were not unknown in high school programs, either then or now. Brown indignantly denied it.

What he referred to as "law and order" was instilled in his players immediately. Before the season began, Brown held a dinner with the players and their parents. It was made clear that any violation of the rules he set down would bring instant dismissal from the team. No drinking. No smoking. No riding around in cars with girls. In fact, no dating at all during the season (which may have been honored more in the breach than the observance). A 9:30 PM curfew, with lights out at 10:00. Parents were given the responsibility of overseeing these restrictions, and, this being Massillon, they took their roles very seriously.

Brown did not hesitate to follow through on his threats. Oddly enough, however, some Massillon boosters could not recall a starter ever getting kicked off the team for a violation.

What also was made clear at these introductory meetings was that there was no color bar at Massillon. The best players played. End of story. Buut Anderson, Edgar Herring, the Gillom brothers, Odell and Horace—at a time when many northern schools were segregated or did not choose to play black athletes, Brown consistently started African Americans.

Horace Gillom was a particular favorite. His older brother, Odell, played end for Massillon in 1935–36, and Horace came along four years later. Horace was an All-State player at the same position as his older brother, but his specialty was punting.

There are two different stories about how he developed that skill. Bud Houghton, who succeeded Brown as Massillon head coach, was in charge of the junior high program when Horace was in the eighth grade. Houghton noticed that it took Gillom an extra step and a half to get the ball off, but once he did he outkicked any punter he ever saw.

According to Houghton, he had Gillom line up 15 yards behind center instead of the usual 10. "The extra five yards didn't make any difference to him," Houghton said. Horace punted that way for the rest of his career, and led the NFL in 1951 and 1952, making the Pro Bowl the latter season.

Brown told a different version of the tale. According to him, no one had taught Gillom the proper punting fundamentals until Brown took him aside after a junior high practice. "When he started doing it the correct way, he became a great punter," Brown said in a written recollection. "In my mind there has never been a better punter than Horace."

Brown may have appeared self-effacing at times, but when it came to his favorite players, he wanted to be given credit.

Gillom was such a favorite of Brown's that when his own son broke his leg as a boy he told his dad, "I bet you're glad it's me and not Horace."

Brown also played the good cop/bad cop routine to perfection. His assistants were aware of their roles in this ongoing drama. Just to keep things sharp when everything was going too smoothly, he would chew out the entire team on the practice field and stalk off. The assistants would then rush in, soothe the players, agree that "the old man" (Brown was barely 30 at this time) may have spoken harshly, but "we have to keep him happy."

By 1934 he had been given the title of athletic director. With centralized control, he could bring all the school's sports programs into his coaching system. His top football assistants, Carroll Widdoes and Hugh McGranahan, handled the actual coaching assignments in the other sports. Widdoes even took the basketball team to the state semifinals three times, losing once in the championship game. But there was never any doubt about which sport ultimately owned Massillon's soul.

The system gave Brown the chance to install a mandatory, year-round conditioning program. His football practices were constantly being refined and broken into ever smaller details, each one intended to cover a specific assignment.

Brown also came up with the idea of playbooks, on which his players would repeatedly be tested. He saw no reason why football shouldn't be viewed as an extension of classroom work. He regarded himself, above all, as a teacher.

He also began the practice of sending in plays from the sidelines to his quarterback through hand signals.

Several Massillon players followed him to Ohio State University and to the Cleveland Browns. They said that the routine never varied. Anyone who played for Brown in high school knew exactly how he would run things with the pros.

Brown recalled how Dave Stewart, the coach he idolized, would take his quarterback to Cedar Point, Ohio, before the season began to get the player's head ready for what lay ahead. Brown's father still owned a small fishing cabin back in Norwalk, Ohio, along the Huron River, and Brown instituted the practice of taking his starters there in August for a similar preparatory getaway.

The 1935 season, with the climactic victory over McKinley, removed the final questions about Brown's coaching abilities. But that was only a prelude. The legend would now build in earnest.

Massillon lost one game in the next five years, when the entire right side of his line came down with the flu at New Castle, Pennsylvania, in 1937 and had to be sent home. Massillon lost 7–0. A furious Brown blamed it solely on overconfidence and redoubled the efforts that went into game preparation.

He felt that his team had become a victim of its own excellence. Sportswriter Luther Emery said that he exchanged heated words with Brown, who accused the newspaper of building up a sense of inevitable victory. Brown also felt that feeling had been transferred to game officials. They had made a close call against Massillon early in the defeat because, he wrote later, they sensed a rout and wanted to keep things close for a while.

Most of all, he blamed himself for inadequately preparing the substitutes for any game situation they might encounter. One of them missed a defensive assignment on a reverse for New Castle's only touchdown. Brown swore that such a lapse would never happen again.

No excuses.

By 1936 Massillon's 7,000-seat stadium had become too small for the program Brown had created. It could not begin to accommodate the hordes who wanted to see their Tigers. He knew that with a larger stadium he could bring in teams from all over the region. Big attractions would mean more money pouring into the school system. Not only to his program but also to an entire range of extracurriculars that could not legally be funded by taxes, from the school choir to the science club.

Brown convinced the school board president Dr. H.W. Bell of the need for a new stadium, and Brown managed to finagle federal funds from the Works Progress Administration (WPA) to acquire land to build a 20,000-seat stadium in the southeastern corner of the city. It opened in 1939, and it is now named for Brown.

Teams from Pennsylvania, Indiana, West Virginia, and as far away as Iowa were soon coming to call. In Ohio, however, Brown's reputation at Massillon was increasingly feared. Between 1935 and 1939, the Tigers' record was 48-1-1. Massillon outscored its opponents 1,916 to 162, or by an average of 38-3.

Massillon's schedule was always heavy with schools from the industrial towns in the northeastern part of the state: Alliance, Akron, Barberton, Warren, Youngstown, Steubenville, even Cleveland, and of course, Canton. Other Ohio schools, however, were wary about sending their teams against Brown's machine. Columbus East High School scheduled him in 1936 and was thrashed 52-0 for its audacity.

When Weir High School of Weirton, West Virginia, was dismembered 48-0 in 1940, its coach, Carl Hamill, wrote a congratulatory note to Brown. He said Massillon was the best high school team he ever had seen and suggested Brown might want to schedule the University of West Virginia instead.

"We have no regrets or alibis," Hamill wrote. "We'll show up and make you play your varsity against us. But if you continue to outclass your opponents, whom are you going to play in years to come? How many teams can give Massillon a good game?"

Actually, Hamill's suggestion about scheduling a college team was not that far-fetched. Brown had arranged a preseason scrimmage with the Kent State University varsity in 1940. The contest was halted when Massillon reached 50 points. Kent went on to win its conference title that season.

Brown felt that his 1940 team could have handled his 1941 squad at Ohio State, too.

But in other parts of Ohio, people were dubious. After all, they argued, this was a terrific football state. There were great high school teams in other big cities, like Cincinnati, Dayton, and Toledo. How would Massillon do against them?

Toledo's Waite High School was among the doubters. In 1939 both schools had ended the season undefeated. No team had come within 27 points of Massillon until the traditional finale with McKinley, and seven of its 10 opponents had been shut out. When the Tigers finished with a 20-6 dispatch of the Bulldogs, they were awarded the state championship for the fifth straight year.

Massillon did not participate in postseason games. So when Waite accepted an invitation to play Portsmouth High in a championship game at Ohio Stadium and won, the Toledo school also claimed the state title.

Through the off-season the pressure built, fueled by media and even school board members in the two cities, for a game between the teams in 1940. Both were expected to repeat as title contenders. Neither school had the same date open on their schedules, though, and it appeared as if the argument simply would go on without resolution. But the challenge was too much for Massillon. It paid off Canton's Lehman High School and opened up the first Friday night in November. Waite would come into Tiger Stadium in return for 40 percent of the gate.

The anticipation was unprecedented. Massillon had won 30 games in a row, and Waite had won 18 straight. If high schools could play games of the century, this would have been it in Ohio. Some commentators felt it was even bigger than Canton McKinley, but that sounded like sacrilege to most fans.

More than 2,500 people had to be turned away from the ticket windows after waiting all morning in a driving rain. Journalists from across Ohio and even neighboring states packed the press box. A Toledo radio station carried the play-by-play description, and a special train with 15 coaches and a dining car was ordered up to bring in the Waite fans.

Emery pointedly observed that Waite outweighed Massillon, and while it had "seen fit to establish itself as the underdog, it still lays claim to the state championship."

There were serious concerns about the size of the Toledo players, particularly their star blocking back, Jack Baker. He weighed 230 pounds and knocked defensive linemen aside as if they were matchsticks. No one had been able to stand up to Waite's ground game, although two of its victories had come by a single touchdown.

"Can the Tiger forward wall throw back Toledo's mighty thrusts?" asked Emery.

There was another element that entered into this game, too. When Massillon played McKinley in 1935, America was still trying to climb out of the Depression. The concerns of most Ohioans then didn't extend much beyond the state's borders. By 1940, though, that all seemed like a long time ago. Most of the world outside America's borders was at war. France had fallen to the Nazi blitzkrieg, and England was trying to stand up to incessant Luftwaffe raids. Italy had declared war on Greece. The heavy drumming in the distance was growing steadily louder, and even in Ohio it could no longer be ignored.

It was announced that Massillon's musical director, George Bird, had prepared a patriotic halftime show, "The History of Democracy," that promised to be almost as stirring as the game itself. Before kickoff the crowd stood and sang "God Bless America." Kate Smith had introduced the song on her radio show two years before, and it already was beloved as a patriotic hymn, almost on the same level as the national anthem.

One thing never changed, though. Football still fully engaged Massillon's passions. Toledo Waite already had established itself as a rival worthy of scorn by choosing to stay overnight in Canton before the big game. It was as if Waite was deliberately allying itself with the Tigers' traditional enemy.

In the end, however, Waite could not hold up. It was limited to one first down all night, and its vaunted ground game was held to 43 yards. Its coach, Jack Mollenkopf, who would later put together great teams at Purdue University, tried to take a page from Brown's 1935 playbook and play an eight-man defensive line. Mollenkopf figured that with the turf and ball soaking wet from the driving rain, Brown's team would not be able to run on them. But the coach's plan could not control the quick, relentless Tigers, who piled up 343 yards on the ground.

Massillon blocked two punts in the first half, one of them when Waite was trying to be ultracautious and kicked on second down. Star running back Tommy James darted in for the touchdown from the 7-yard line. Another blocked punt rolled out of the Waite end zone for a safety.

The score remained 8–0 at the half, but still Waite could not move against Brown's defense. James scored again in the third quarter, and then Ray Getz broke loose on a 48-yard run to put it away.

Brown had put up a sign in the Massillon locker room that read: "The team that gets the first 6 inches wins the ballgame." During the course of this game the Massillon line consistently won this battle of inches by getting the first 12.

The joy in Massillon knew no limits.

"Still Laying Claim to a State Title, Waite?" read the gloating page-one headline in the *Independent* on Saturday.

"Waite might be tough in the northwest section of the state," said the game story, "but around here it's just another team."

One Massillon reporter had prepared a summary of the game stats to present to the Toledo school board member who had most vocally claimed Waite's right to the title. "But he was nowhere to be found," chortled this paragon of objective journalism.

The last two games on the 1940 schedule were anticlimactic. Even when McKinley shocked the Tigers by scoring first in the traditional contest—the first points Massillon had given up all year—the team easily came back to control the game. It throttled Canton for the sixth straight time, 34–6.

This 1940 Massillon team is still regarded by most historians as the greatest in Ohio high school athletics, unlikely ever to be matched.

"There wasn't that much competition for top athletes from the Catholic schools back then," says team historian Junie Studer, "and a whole new high school has been built in the area that used to be part of the Massillon district. It'll never be like it was."

The *Independent* unhesitatingly called the Waite game "the most decisive triumph of [Brown's] career."

But it was a career that had almost run its course in Massillon. On the same sports page that carried the story of the victory over Waite, a small news item indicated that Ohio State University was looking to hire the great University of Pittsburgh football coach, Jock Sutherland.

Everyone knew a shake-up was coming in Columbus. But no one guessed how it would rock Massillon, too.

5

1941: Ohio State University 20, University of Michigan 20

If Brown's alma mater, Miami University, would become known as the "cradle of coaches," by 1940 Ohio State University was getting a reputation as their graveyard. That was a trifle unfair. Since joining the Western Conference (the formal name of the Big Ten) in 1913, the Buckeyes had hired only three coaches. The first, however, was Dr. John Wilce, and he was an icon beyond reproach.

Wilce came to Columbus at the age of 25, after a fine athletic career at the University of Wisconsin, and was credited with taking Ohio State football to national prominence. During his 16-year tenure, OSU won three conference championships, beat the University of Michigan for the first time, built the massive horseshoe of Ohio Stadium, developed its first All-American superstar in Chic Harley, and truly became the entire state's team. Even the school's fight song, "Across the Field," was written as a tribute to him.

After the 1928 season, Wilce announced that he would retire to practice medicine. He returned to the university in later years and became director of health services. His accomplishments, his move to a higher calling, and the fact that he left under his own steam gave Wilce a certain niche in Columbus.

Then things got strange.

Wilce's replacement was Sam Willaman, his top assistant and the first Ohio State grad to hold the job. Willaman seemed to be doing fine. His overall record was, in fact, better than Wilce's. Willaman's last two teams, in 1932 and 1933, lost only two games in the Big Ten. Unfortunately, they were both to Michigan.

In 1933 he went 7-1, shut out five opponents, and finished second in the conference. But he faltered at Ann Arbor, 13-0, and when the season ended, he decided to escape the rising chorus of abuse and take the coaching job at Western Reserve University, a rather steep step down.

Replacing him was Francis Schmidt, a hearty former attorney who favored vests and bow ties. Schmidt had run up an excellent record at Texas Christian University and introduced a highly complex offense featuring plenty of laterals and multiple fakes. The press quickly named it "razzle dazzle."

But Schmidt most endeared himself to Columbus by introducing one of the great sports clichés of all time. When asked how he would handle Michigan, he responded: "What's so special about Michigan? They put on their pants one leg at a time like everyone else."

Then he went out and walloped the Wolverines two straight years, 34-0 and 38-0. Those were the biggest victory margins for Ohio State in the history of the series. Delirious Buckeyes fans began the tradition of awarding tiny tokens of golden pants to the members of teams that beat Michigan.

Schmidt accumulated two more pairs of tiny golden pants by shutting out Michigan again, by scores of 21-0 both times.

Tales grew around him, celebrating Schmidt as sort of an absent-minded genius. In one such story, he was lost in thought when he took his car in for repairs. He chose to stay inside when it was put up on a hoist. Suddenly snapping out of his reverie, he swung the door open, exited the vehicle...and fell to the floor of the garage. Only his beefy frame enabled him to avoid injury.

Then it all turned around. Michigan brought in its own coaching genius, Fritz Crisler, and with him came All-American halfback Tom Harmon. The Wolverines beat Schmidt's Buckeyes three straight times. When the 1940 team came into Columbus and mauled Ohio State 40-0, Schmidt was toast.

Now it seemed to the boosters that his conditioning program was too lax, his defense too slow, and other teams had caught on to his offensive tricks. Within days he was out and moving on to Idaho, another downward progression.

Paul Brown was a spectator at the final debacle in Ohio Stadium. There was open speculation well before the Michigan game that Schmidt was gone. Brown had heard it. He was also aware of the rising insistence among members of the Ohio Football Coaches Association that Schmidt be replaced by one of their own. Unquestionably, they felt that someone should be Brown—the "Miracle Man of Massillon," as he was now known.

There were dissenters. Many complained that the leap from high school to a big-time college program was simply too great—forgetting that was exactly what the revered Wilce had done 27 years prior.

Ohio State Athletic Director Lynn St. John heard arguments from both sides and decided to travel to Massillon to size up this 33-year-old coaching prodigy for himself. It was a familiar path for someone from the Ohio State football operation. Brown noted with amusement that his high school teams were more thoroughly scouted by Ohio assistants and recruiters than many of their college opponents.

There was no denying Brown wanted the job. Even though Ohio State turned him away as a player, the dream had never died. He had accomplished all he could at Massillon after getting the job he never imagined could be his. Now the golden path to Columbus seemed to be clearing for him, too.

At times, Brown would say that he had "no vision beyond Massillon. It was the grandest prospect possible." But he knew that wasn't true. In his own ghostwritten biography he says that "coaching the Buckeyes was my ultimate dream."

The chief candidate for the job was supposed to be Don Faurot, the head coach at University of Missouri and a great offensive innovator. St. John knew, however, that denying Brown the job would have severe repercussions in Ohio. Michigan and Purdue University recruited heavily in the state, and it rankled Ohio State, which wanted to keep these players at home and was not eager to offend the state's coaches, who had a major influence on players' choice of a school.

Massillon school board president H.W. Bell thought Brown should take the job, but he repeated his earlier warning about Brown being "wound too tight" for it. The coach was well aware of his own single-mindedness. Some called it obsessiveness. In Brown's mind that was a virtue. He enjoyed playing cards and the piano and, in later years, golf. But in football season there was just one thing he would permit to occupy his mind.

Sure, Massillon was tough and at Ohio State the entire state would be his campus, to cheer or condemn him. Willaman and Schmidt had learned that lesson to their sorrow. But Brown welcomed it.

St. John began meeting with him secretly at the home of a mutual acquaintance in Wooster, Ohio. Brown said later that football was almost never discussed. Issues of character and philosophy toward athletics and family were the main topics of conversation.

Ohio State in 1941 was a conservative campus in a conservative state. Humorist James Thurber and fellow Ohio State alumnus Elliot Nugent had depicted it in the 1940 Broadway hit, *The Male Animal*, as a place where football would always trump academic freedom. It was unfair (although not entirely so at that time), but it shaped the national perception of Ohio State as a football factory.

It seems precious in this era of million-dollar coaching salaries, thuggish behavior by athletes, recruiting malfeasances, and massive television contracts for bowl appearances to speak seriously of character. But in 1941 the Big Ten viewed itself in these terms. (Actually, it was only the Big 9 then. The University of Chicago had dropped varsity football in 1939, and Michigan State University would not join to round out the number until 1953.)

Teams played only an eight-game schedule, sometimes not starting until October. Bowl games were out of the question. The Big Ten felt it did not need such a distraction. Nor did it feel any compulsion to prove its excellence against other conferences. It was fully aware of its own superiority.

Ivy League schools such as Dartmouth College and Cornell University were still ranked high in the polls. Athletes did not receive full scholarships but were expected, instead, to earn money by working at off-season jobs provided by boosters, a practice that would become massively abused by the 1950s.

Brown was offered an annual salary of $6,500 to come to Ohio State, approximately $1,500 more than he had been making at Massillon. That wasn't bad money in 1941. Figured in today's dollars it was more like $75,000. Still that's a far cry from what a Jim Tressel makes today, when TV contracts and endorsements are figured in. There were, of course, no such things back then.

Brown joked later that much of the enthusiasm of the high school coaches' association to snag him the Ohio State job was "to get me out of the way." But there was also a sense that Schmidt's tenure was an aberration. The Ohio State job should belong to an Ohio man.

The announcement was made in January 1941, with the roads so icy that he couldn't drive back to Massillon to tell his family in person. But news like that got out fast, and it was the stuff of banner headlines on the state's sports pages. The (Cleveland) Plain Dealer took a familiar tack: "Another Wilce? Buck Fans Hope They Found One in Brown." There were pictures of him holding a football, with his family, diagramming a play for St. John.

"He has absolute conviction and supreme confidence that he can do the job required," wrote the paper's beat writer, John Dietrich. "He believes Columbus townspeople and newspapermen are strictly normal, not a den of wolves."

The same paper's editorial page sounded a more skeptical note: "The Ohio State athletic board does the unusual in selecting a head coach not only without previous experience in college football, but without previous contacts with big-time football. We hope for Brown's sake that the Ohio State alumni who were behind his appointment will not expect him to continue with unbeaten teams in the Big Ten.... The need is less for a new head coach than for a master of line play."

But The Plain Dealer's editorial writers couldn't have been more mistaken. Brown was in constant contact with big-time programs. Their recruiters were always buzzing around Massillon. He knew how that game was played.

"I was no babe in the woods," he said about himself. But he took a more self-effacing tone when meeting with the press at the official announcement.

"My chief hope is that I can wear well," he said. Brown said that to play for him a young man had to be "brave, smart, and fast. Our job is to build a winning attitude, to get them in shape. I don't want them too beefy, but they must be ready to go 60 minutes, like Harmon."

He knew where to find such players. Six of them came from his 1940 Massillon team, including All-State players Horace Gillom and Tommy James. Brown sat down with them and made it clear that they would not get special consideration in Columbus. But that was malarkey, and they knew it. They already understood Brown's system and methods, and that would be invaluable to him at Ohio State.

Brown's friends in the coaches' association also persuaded two promising athletes who were considering other offers to change their minds and play for Brown. Dante Lavelli and Bill Willis not only came to Ohio State, they went on become essential ingredients in the making of the Cleveland Browns, too.

"His influence is almost hypnotic," wrote an enthused Dietrich. "Ninety percent of the state believes that his regime will be an instantaneous and overwhelming success because everyone in Ohio is behind it."

But Brown knew what he was facing. He was coming into a situation much like he had encountered at Massillon nine years before. A great program had been allowed to deteriorate, and the first task would be to rebuild its spirit.

Under Schmidt, the Buckeyes had finished one-two in the Big Ten, with a winning record for every year but the last one. They were sixth in the Associated Press Poll before the 1939 Michigan game, the highest the Buckeyes had been ranked since polling was instituted in 1936.

But the 1940 team had gone 4–4 and lost three conference games. To Brown's eye the team was poorly conditioned and insufficiently coached in the small, vital details of their individual assignments. Brown's system depended on every player clearly understanding his role in every play in his book. Coaches would work separately with the guards or tackles, not with the entire line, and each man would be repeatedly drilled and quizzed.

Brown also began working with the freshman team, using the same system he had put in place at the junior high in Massillon. Freshmen were slotted by position to fill the next year's needs on the varsity so that Brown would never find himself with a hole left unfilled by a graduating senior.

Schmidt believed that trickery could make up for a lack of speed. Brown dismissed such an idea as preposterous. Nothing could make up for a lack of speed. But Brown also was convinced, contrary to the cliché, that speed can be coached.

"A 250-pound lineman cannot run with a halfback," he said. "But if he masters the fundamentals of running, he can lessen the distance."

Brown had studied the running technique and theories of Ohio State's great Olympian, Jesse Owens, and was convinced that they could be adapted to football players. It was also Brown who adopted the 40-yard dash as a measure of speed because he figured that's how far a player would have to run downfield to cover a punt.

He adopted "lean and hungry" as the team motto and insisted that some of his linemen drop 20 pounds. He kept telling them, "The she-wolf fights best on an empty stomach."

He also was satisfied with his lineup of Ohio boys, rock hard from working on farms or before the furnaces of the steel mills, instilled with the proper work ethic, and properly educated and coachable. With such men, Brown felt he could compete with anyone. Especially Michigan.

The Ann Arbor school had gone through a fallow period coinciding with Schmidt's early years in Columbus. Since 1900, Michigan had compiled a winning season in all but six years—and four of those years fell between 1934 and 1937. With the arrival of Crisler, however, the Wolverines were once again formidable.

The two teams moved their meeting to the last game of the season in 1935, where it has remained, except for one memorable year, ever since. Always a big game, its position as the season's climax has raised it to gargantuan proportions at both schools. *Sports Illustrated* calls it the greatest collegiate rivalry of all.

Brown saw the record. He knew that whatever else he accomplished at OSU, he would be judged on the Michigan game.

Michigan finished the 1940 season ranked number three, two notches behind the national champions of Minnesota. Its pasting of Ohio State in the season finale had moved Michigan up four places in the final poll, which made it rankle even more.

Harmon was gone in 1941, but the team was still a cofavorite with Minnesota to win the conference. Michigan's captain, Bob Westfall, was regarded as nearly Harmon's equal. Its defensive front, anchored by Al Wistert and Merv Pregulman, may have been the best in the country.

Brown was well schooled in preparing for a big game. He had learned all about that at Massillon. So building the Buckeyes up to a peak for Michigan was almost business as usual for him. Almost. There were considerable hurdles to clear before that happened.

As luck would have it, the 1941 Ohio State opener was against Missouri. Its coach was Faurot, the other top candidate for the job Brown landed. Although Faurot would go on to a long career at Mizzou—the football stadium there is named for him—he was miffed at having been passed over. He arrived in Columbus with a little surprise for the Buckeyes: a newly installed split-T formation.

This would become a standard offensive set. It would go on to open up college football and became the basis for the quarterback option attack. But in September 1941, it was revolutionary. The underdog Missouri team began the first quarter by ripping huge holes in the Ohio State front, and panic quickly started to seep into the enterprise. Brown called it "one of the worst moments of my coaching career."

While Missouri spread its offense across the field, Brown coolly instructed his defense to maintain its regular spacing. That enabled the confused Ohio State players to continue working within their familiar assignments, and while Missouri reeled off big yardage between the 20-

yard lines, the attack bogged down near the Buckeyes goal lines. The offense was still new to the Missouri players, too, and they did not know how to run it smoothly when the field shortened.

The Buckeyes came away with a 12–7 win in Brown's debut, and he knew how narrowly he had averted a catastrophe. Missouri swept through the rest of its schedule, losing again only in a bowl game, 2–0, on a field that was muddy slop. But the Ohio State–Missouri game was not supposed to have been this close, and some of the more avid Ohio State fans grumbled. They knew Brown's reputation, and they wanted blowouts. They also did not quite understand what they had just seen.

Brown had always preached that "poise under stress" was the defining moment of a great athlete. His coolness in the face of the unexpected against Missouri deeply impressed football minds in Ohio and across the nation.

Then the team hopped a train for the West Coast and beat Southern California, 33–0—the first time the Buckeyes ever had won a game in California. So the excitement began to build again.

Even a tough 14–7 loss to Northwestern in the fourth week couldn't dull the luster. It was the first football game Brown had lost in four years, after 36 consecutive wins. But he came away with something useful, something he saw that day. Brown was always a close observer of opposing players, hoping to spot a weakness that hadn't turned up in the films and could be exploited. But he left this game with an admiration for the incredible peripheral vision of the player who had defeated him, the Wildcats' sophomore tailback. His name was Otto Graham.

When the Buckeyes got back on track the following week by defeating Pittsburgh, yet another player came to his attention. The Panthers' speedy tailback, Edgar Jones, was nicknamed "Special Delivery" for obvious reasons. Brown liked his speed and shiftiness and his willingness to take a hit. He, too, would soon figure in Brown's scheme.

The Buckeyes ripped past Wisconsin and Illinois and rose to the number-14 ranking in the polls. Then it was Michigan.

In those years, the Big Ten only scheduled five or six conference games. Ohio State was 3–1 but did not play defending champion University of Minnesota, the only team to have beaten Michigan.

In other games against common opponents, including Northwestern University, the Wolverines had won by impressive margins. Going into the Ohio State game, Michigan was ranked fifth in the country, and with the game being played in Ann Arbor, it was a two-touchdown favorite.

Syndicated columnist John Lardner offered a rhymed prediction about this game:

> Michigan will cut the giblets
> Out of poor Ohio State.
> (Kids who play at railroad crossings
> Are conceding too much weight.)

But the beat reporters who had watched Brown for an entire season suspected that he had something planned and was shrewdly keeping it under wraps. They had become convinced that the Miracle Man would always come up with a surprise. Dietrich even went so far as to write, "OSU may win." But he quickly tempered that by saying, "Win, lose, or draw, Brown has made an excellent showing."

Dietrich's instincts were correct, though. Brown and his defensive coach, Fritz Mackey, had broken down the Michigan offensive scheme. It relied on trap blocking to slow down the defensive rush before it could disrupt the series of fakes the Wolverines ran in the backfield. But what if Ohio State used a five-man front and brought up a linebacker to blitz the weak side of the Michigan line? That could throw off Michigan's blocking scheme just enough to give the Buckeyes the advantage of the unexpected.

Brown understood that this shift alone wasn't enough. He made sure the team was reminded of the previous year's calamity, even spreading out the stat sheet from that game in the team's hotel when it was printed in a Detroit paper. He also posted one of his favorite slogans in the locker room: "If we die, we die by inches." Ohio State would not go down without fighting for every measure of territory on the field.

In 1968, after an underdog Harvard team scored 16 points in the last 42 seconds of the game, the headline in the next edition of *The Harvard Crimson* read: "Harvard Beats Yale, 29-29."

That was pretty much the reaction in Ohio after the 1941 Michigan game. The Wolverines ran up 375 yards and punted only three times. But Brown's unorthodox defense turned them away time after time at the Ohio State goal line.

Michigan finally managed to pull ahead, 14-7, in the third quarter. But OSU tailback Jack Graf led the Buckeyes on a 65-yard drive to even it up again.

Back came Michigan, with Westfall and tailback Tom Kuzma leading the charge downfield. But again the Ohio State defense held, this time at its own 4-yard line.

The Buckeyes then went off on a stirring 96-yard expedition. Halfback Dick Fisher, used as a decoy for the entire game, broke into the clear from the Michigan 45, and Graf hit him in stride for the touchdown. The kick was missed, but Ohio State led 20-14 with 13 minutes to play. Michigan had only given up 21 points all season coming into this game, and OSU had nearly doubled that.

But the Buckeyes were physically exhausted and couldn't hold off the Wolverines any longer. On a six-and-a-half minute drive, Michigan punched it in once more.

In the long-ago Michigan game that Brown had watched as a college freshman at Ohio Stadium, the Buckeyes fell short of a major upset by missing an extra point. Now here it was again, with Brown's own team facing the same disappointment.

The standard practice in football today is to freeze the opponent's place kicker by calling consecutive timeouts. That's what Brown did.

"Everyone thought I was trying to psych (the kicker) out," he said later. "But that wasn't it. After the way our boys had fought, I just couldn't bear to watch them lose like this. So I wanted to avert the inevitable for as long as possible."

Whatever the motivation, the conversion failed, and it was 20-20.

There was still 6:40 to play, though, and Brown dreaded the thought of putting the ball back in Michigan's hands again. In an audacious gamble that he never fully explained, he went for the yardage on fourth down at the Ohio 45. And he fell short.

But the supposedly spent Buckeyes defense had one more stop left in it, and when a Westfall pass was intercepted a few seconds later, the game was decided.

As far as the state of Ohio was concerned, the Buckeyes had won, 20–20. The governor even had a commemorative license plate printed up for Brown. It read PB-20, and he kept it on his cars for the next 22 years.

Brown spent the next week duck hunting on the Lake Erie shore and thinking about the promising sophomore class that would be coming in for the 1942 season.

But 15 days after this game was played, Pearl Harbor was attacked. And everything changed.

6

1942: Ohio State University 21, University of Michigan 7

When the two great rivals met again, America was a nation at war. But the biggest number of draft call-ups were still in the future, and for most of 1942 the same familiar faces remained on the sports pages. Indeed, when Detroit slugger Hank Greenberg actually enlisted in the Army it was regarded as an act worthy of commendation on editorial pages.

At the time, the 1942 Rose Bowl had been played in Durham, North Carolina, because of invasion scares in California following the attack on Pearl Harbor. There were travel restrictions in effect, and there was gasoline rationing. As a result, attendance at most sporting events plummeted. At Ann Arbor, Michigan, for example, only 17,000 people showed up for the opening game of the University of Michigan's season.

But the war affected more than just attendance. The Big Ten schedule had been expanded from eight to 10 games so that teams from military training bases could be fit in. Ohio State would open the season against Fort Knox and close it with Iowa Pre-Flight, in addition to six conference games and matches with the University of Southern California and the University of Pittsburgh.

Coach Paul Brown felt that he was putting on another man's clothes when he arrived in Columbus in 1941. While he had accomplished more than anyone had expected, he had never felt entirely comfortable with the team he inherited from Schmidt. This year, however, the pipeline was sending forth his own recruits, his personally selected men. His sophomore class was brilliant, led by Bill Willis, Dante Lavelli, and fullback Gene Fekete. James and George Slusser checked in from Massillon Washington High School. Returning half-back Les Horvath was an All-American in the making. Junior Lin Houston had also played for Brown at Massillon and was his ideal line-man, a guard who was almost as fast as a halfback. Don McCafferty, who would later coach the Baltimore Colts to a Super Bowl victory, was a starter at tackle. Only three starters were coming back from the 1941 squad, and there was uncertainty in the press as to how this would play out over the season. Brown, however, knew he had the team he wanted: overwhelming team speed and a roster filled with "my kind of guy, (who) says a little and does a lot."

When the Buckeyes blasted Fort Knox 59-0 in the opener, it almost felt like watching Massillon again. Then Ohio State followed up their first game with decisive wins over Southern California and Indiana University, and when the first Associated Press Poll of the season was released on October 12, there were the Buckeyes at number one. It was the first time in history they had been ranked there.

The Associated Press Poll of sportswriters had been instituted six years prior as a circulation gimmick. Then, as now, the results were often open to question. The previous season, for example, after tying Michigan and finishing with the same overall record as the Wolverines, Ohio State ended up ranked 13th in the final poll, while Michigan was fifth.

The selection of Texas Christian University and Texas A&M University as national champions in 1938 and 1939 also touched off heated arguments. It was understood that the Southwest Conference did not measure up to the kind of football played in the Midwest and East—at least, that was how it was understood in the East and Midwest. The Big Ten, Notre Dame University, and the service academies also did not participate in bowl games.

The University of Minnesota had won the title three of the six years the polling was conducted, and there had been little dispute about that. But Ohio State really was not thinking of a national title.

Winning the Big Ten, as always, was its most important goal. Still, there it was, number one.

The team went on to blank Purdue University and got back at Northwestern University for the previous season's only loss. The Bucks were 5-0 and headed to Madison, Wisconsin, to play a very tough University of Wisconsin team. The Badgers had fought Notre Dame to a tie and were otherwise unblemished.

Then the war came home to Brown and the Bucks. Football teams were no exception to the travel restrictions. The best railroad equipment was reserved to carry troops and war material. Everyone else had to scramble.

Ohio State played only three road games all year, and this was the longest haul. The team made the trip in antique coaches that appeared to have been sitting on some remote sidetrack for the last several years. Among the things that hadn't been cleaned was the water supply. Members of the team who drank from it were violently ill by the time they reached Wisconsin.

For Brown it was almost a repeat of his 1937 loss on the road with Massillon, when half the team came down with the flu and had to be sent home.

"When we went to the stadium to get dressed, half the boys were so sick all they could do was stretch out on the floor in their uniforms," he said. "It affected my coaches the same way."

A tough game had turned into an impossibility. Wisconsin won 17-7. By the next Monday, OSU had dropped to sixth in the polls. The AP didn't factor bad water into the voting.

But once more Brown had the team pointed toward the big finish. And Horvath had arrived as a superstar.

He had grown up in the Cleveland suburb of Parma, but said later that his family rented a home in the city so he could play high school football there. "Before a basketball game I heard my teammates at Parma High talking about a party they were going to that night," he recalled later. "It seemed to me they just weren't taking the game seriously enough, so I told my parents and we relocated overnight."

Horvath was a rather slight young man, weighing 160 pounds or so, with great speed and a strong arm. He was regarded as the fastest man in the Big Ten at that time.

"The only bad thing about Les is that he wasn't very big," said Jack Graf, his teammate in 1941. "But he was very quick, and he used his brains to make up for his lack of size."

Fekete called him a "feisty runner." "When defenders got hold of him, though, he got a pretty good lick. Both of us also spoke Hungarian. So whenever we were talking on the field and didn't want anyone else to know what we were saying, that's what we spoke. It used to drive everyone else nuts. Sometimes we'd even yell at the refs in Hungarian."

"He was the best player of our day," said Willis. "He could never bull you over, so he had to elude you. There weren't many people who were able to catch him."

Horvath was a serious student, too, in a predentistry course of study.

With Paul Sarringhaus, who outweighed Horvath by 55 pounds, as the other halfback, Brown felt he had an unstoppable backfield combination. Going into the Michigan game at 7-1, this team already scored 275 points, more than any other Ohio State team had ever run up over an eight-game season.

They rolled over Pittsburgh 59-19, with Horvath averaging eight yards per carry. The Illinois game was moved to Cleveland, so fans in Ohio's largest city could get a look at Brown's Buckeyes and their hometown hero, Horvath.

The huge lakefront stadium also was packed with fans from both Massillon and Canton—cheering together for once in a common cause. Ohio State plastered the Illini 44-20, and Horvath sent everyone home happy by scoring two touchdowns and passing for another.

The newspapers had taken to calling the team the "Scarlet Scourge." But the real test was at hand.

Michigan started the season slowly, with a loss to Iowa Pre-Flight and another to its nemesis, Minnesota. But the week before the Ohio State game, it had gone into South Bend and, in front of a capacity crowd, knocked off a favored Notre Dame team, 32-20.

"The Michigan win caused no more alarm in Columbus than a bona-fide air raid alert," wrote a Cleveland columnist. "Buckeye supporters didn't think the Wolverines were that good." Despite having the better record, Ohio State was ranked fifth in the AP Poll and Michigan fourth. The Wolverines were installed as a three-point favorite.

Wisconsin stumbled the week after it defeated the Buckeyes and lost to Iowa. So Ohio State, by virtue of playing one more conference game than the Badgers, would take the Big Ten title if it won the next game.

Gas rationing or no, Buckeye fans could not miss this one. The horseshoe-shaped Ohio Stadium was filled to near capacity for the date.

The national title seemed out of reach. The University of Georgia, Georgia Tech, and Boston College were all undefeated. The two Georgia teams were to meet the following week, and the winner of that game would be named national champions. In case that didn't work out, Boston College would finish its season against a weak traditional rival, Holy Cross.

But all that seemed inconsequential. Tailback Tommy James, another of Ohio State's backfield burners, had to leave the Illinois game with an injury. As the week went on, the medical reports sounded less promising. On Thursday it was announced that Slusser would start in his place and that it was doubtful if James would play at all.

"The very worst thing we can get is a licking," shrugged Brown. "The boys know what they're up against, and they're playing out the string."

A statement like that from Brown was for public consumption. Privately he knew better. With a problem at running back, Ohio State would take to the air. He had every confidence that Michigan would never expect the sort of passing attack he planned to unleash, and even a muddy field couldn't contain it.

After a blocked punt in the second quarter, Horvath hit Sarringhaus with a 35-yard touchdown pass. In the second half, end Bob Shaw managed to get behind Tom Kuzma in the Michigan secondary. Barely keeping his balance along the sidelines, Shaw caught Sarringhaus's pass and went all the way on a 60-yard score. It was Ohio State in the lead with 14-0.

But these games are never easy. Michigan finally found its punch, and led by the running of future All-American Bob Chappuis, the Wolverines drove 64 yards to cut the lead to 14-7. Then in the fourth quarter Michigan fumbled on its own side of the field. This time it was Sarringhaus who found Horvath for the 32-yard touchdown pass.

That was it. There was no comeback left in the Wolverines.

Brown was carried off the field as delirious Ohio State fans cheered what the press box was describing as "the most tremendous victory recorded anywhere in the nation."

Even the coach, his clothes smeared with mud, seemed to be overwhelmed at what had been achieved.

"I can hardly believe it," he said. "We laid our plans for today's peak and we hit it. Michigan's misfortune was that it seemed to reach its peak a week ago. But I'd rather beat them than any other game."

"The greatest football team Ohio State ever had—and the greatest in the country—today reigns as 1942 champions of the Big Ten," exulted *The Plain Dealer*.

The Plain Dealer's editorial page, which had expressed grave reservations over the wisdom of Brown's appointment just 22 months before, could barely restrain itself. "We have to be neutral in the Canton-Massillon affair," it said, "but not so in respect to Ohio State. That is our team, and Paul Brown is our man.... Under a less skilled man, Ohio State might have lost four or five games."

Brown understood exactly what the stakes really were. Fritz Crisler was recruiting heavily in Ohio. Another win by Michigan would have made Crisler's program even more attractive to many of the state's top athletes. But with this victory, Brown had become a heroic figure in Ohio, and his enhanced stature was sure to bring the best to Columbus.

"There were two people responsible for the boost in national recognition OSU received," said Willis in later years. "Paul Brown and Les Horvath. Before those two individuals, Ohio State was not recognized the way it is today."

Something astonishing also occurred in Columbus, Georgia, on this same afternoon. A rather ordinary Auburn University team rose up and smashed undefeated Georgia by two touchdowns. This was an interesting development. But in Ohio's Columbus, in the midst of the post-Michigan euphoria, there was the jarring realization that more work needed to be done.

For the only time since 1935, Michigan was not the last game on Ohio State's regular schedule. The Big Ten title had been clinched, but a loss to Iowa Pre-Flight in this unusual finale would bring the entire season down a note.

The game against the Iowa Pre-Flight Seahawks was no walkover, anything but. Several of the teams assembled at military training bases were as good as or better than the top college squads. Iowa, in particular, started a pack of college stars. (The Seahawks were based in Iowa City and shared some facilities with the University of Iowa, but the athletic teams were entirely separate.)

Forrest Evashevski, quarterback on the Tom Harmon Michigan teams, was there. So was Dick Fisher, who had played a major role for Ohio State in the previous season's 20–20 tie with Michigan.

The Seahawks were coached by Bernie Bierman, who had guided Minnesota to national titles in the previous two years. He had brought along two of his stars, tackle Clayton Tonnemaker and running back Bill Daley. They had handled Michigan by two touchdowns. In fact, their record against the Big Ten was 4–0. Only Notre Dame had managed to beat them.

But Brown was sure that having come this far, the Buckeyes would not let him down. "I like November teams," he said. "Teams that come back late in the season and just won't quit."

He was confident that's what he had here. His team wouldn't need any further goading to take care of this final piece of business on the last Saturday in November. He was right. Ohio State's incredible team speed could not be handled by the bigger, more experienced, but slower, Iowa Pre-Flight.

Bierman thought that Fekete running up the middle was the key to OSU's attack. Actually, he was on to something. Brown liked to use the fullback on all his teams to tighten up the linebackers on opposing defenses and make space for his passing. It was the scheme he would employ with devastating effect with the Cleveland Browns. But Bierman's defense was simply not fast enough to react when Brown's players started running wide.

James, fully recovered from his injury, bounced to the outside and ran 54 yards on the first play from scrimmage. Later he scored on a long punt return. Then Horvath and Sarringhaus went into their interchangeable passing attack that had riddled Michigan.

The Buckeyes trampled the Seahawks, 41–12.

On that same afternoon, Georgia ran over Georgia Tech, 34–0, while Holy Cross destroyed the championship hopes of Boston with an astonishing 55–12 massacre.

University of Tulsa finished undefeated, but it played in the Missouri Valley Conference, which was regarded as a lightweight grouping. Georgia had finished with one loss and could make a case for a championship; especially after it went on to shut out UCLA in the Rose Bowl. But a team from the Deep South wouldn't be voted the Associated Press title until Tennessee made it in 1951. All things being equal, the writers always gave the edge to a Big Ten team.

Ohio State had its national championship, the first in school history. In his second year in Columbus, Brown had conquered college football, just as he had the high school world in Massillon.

A final footnote: on the same afternoon that Ohio State beat Michigan, Massillon fell to Canton McKinley High School, 35–0. That ended the Tigers' 52-game unbeaten streak, as well as the string of seven straight victories over its greatest rival.

It also seemed to symbolize the closing of a chapter in Brown's life; the high school dynasty he had created was ending just as he had scaled the peak of college football.

But the view from the peak was brief. The next year he would get an unaccustomed look at the deepest valley.

A poster for 1917 game pitting Jim Thorpe and the Canton Bulldogs vs. the Massillon Tigers on November 25, 1917. The rivalry between Canton and Massillon served as a perfect launching point for Paul Brown's illustrious career.

Paul Brown (left), football coach at Washington High School in Massillon, Ohio, outlines one of his favorite plays for Lynn W. St. John, Ohio State University athletic director, December 29, 1940.

Brown became the head coach of the Ohio State Buckeyes in 1941. The team, pictured here, tied for second place in the Western Conference. PHOTO COURTESY OF OHIO STATE UNIVERSITY.

Brown, shown here surrounded by members of the 1942 Ohio State University squad, led the Buckeyes to a National Championship in his second season as head coach. PHOTO COURTESY OF OHIO STATE UNIVERSITY.

The Buckeye's passing attack in 1942 handily defeated the Michigan Wolverines and turned Ohio State into Big Ten champions. PHOTO COURTESY OF OHIO STATE UNIVERSITY.

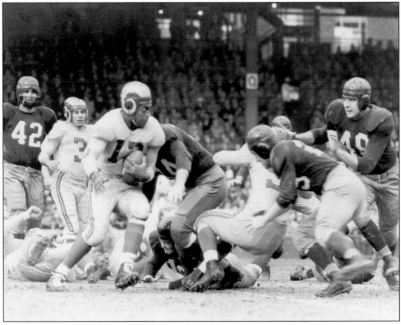

Los Angeles Rams running back Les Horvath, Brown's first All-American at Ohio State, carries in a 41–13 win over the Washington Redskins on December 5, 1948 at Griffith Stadium in Washington, D.C.

Hall of Fame linebacker Marion Motley (76) of the Cleveland Browns tackles the Los Angeles Dons Chuck Fenenbock for a 17–16 win over the Cleveland Browns during an All-America Football Conference game on November 3, 1946 in L.A. Helping Motley are teammates Tom Golelia (92) and Lou Saban (66).

Fullback Marion Motley of the Cleveland Browns. PHOTO BY NFL/NFL

Bill Willis was small by pro football standards in 1946, yet he performed in a class by himself, particularly on defense. In the eight years he played for the Cleveland Browns from 1946 through 1953, he was a first-team All-League selection seven times and a second-team choice once. He also played in three NFL Pro Bowls.

Brown diagrams one of his pass plays on the blackboard in Cleveland on September 26, 1947.

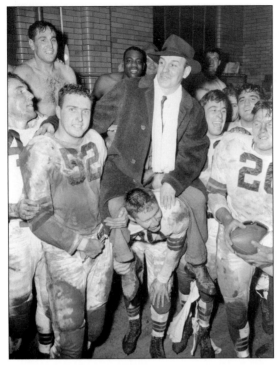

The Cleveland Browns, All-America Football Conference champs, lift their coach, Paul Brown, onto their shoulders after defeating the San Francisco 49ers, 21–7, in Cleveland, December 11, 1949. From left to right, the players are: Lou Rymkus (44), tackle; George Young (52), end; Edgar Jones, halfback, holding Brown; Lou Saban (20), center. Looking over Saban's shoulder are Alex Agase, guard, and Bob Gaudio, guard (right). In back are, left to right: Lou Groza, tackle; and Horace Gillom, tackle.

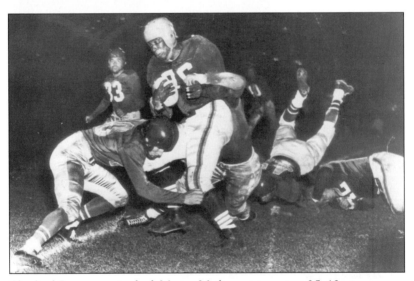

Cleveland Browns running back Marion Motley on a carry in a 35–10 win over the Philadelphia Eagles on September 16, 1950 at Shibe Park in Philadelphia, Pennsylvania. PHOTO BY PRO FOOTBALL HALL OF FAME/NFL

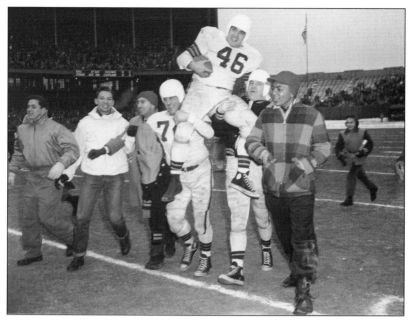

Lou "the Toe" Groza (no. 46) is carried off the field by teammates Tony Adamle, left, and John Kissell and jubilant fans after kicking two field goals to lead the Browns to an 8 to 3 victory over the New York Giants at Cleveland, Ohio, December 17, 1950.

Paul Brown holds up the foot of kicker Lou Groza following the Browns 30–28 victory over the Los Angeles Rams on December 24, 1950.

Coach Paul Brown, wearing baseball cap at lower left, poses with Cleveland Browns players, December 23, 1952. At front, left to right: Coach Brown, Dante Lavelli, Lin Houston, Frank Gatski, and George Young. Standing, left to right: Marion Motley, Otto Graham, Mac Speedie, Lou Groza, and Bill Willis.

Hall of Fame wide receiver Dante Lavelli of the Cleveland Browns makes a catch and chased by Rex Berry in a 23 to 21 win over the San Francisco 49ers on November 15, 1953.

7

1943–1945: Interregnum

In his previous 13 years as a coach, Paul Brown had lost exactly a dozen games. Only three of them were suffered after 1934. But now, because of global circumstances beyond his control, he was about to taste the most bitter of seasons, one that would alter the shape of his career. He watched helplessly as his young and outmanned Ohio State team, depleted by the military draft, struggled to a 3–6 season.

Most of this was because of an odd variance in regulations between the two branches of the military. The navy not only fielded great teams with enlistees at its training bases but allowed athletes in affiliated university programs to compete, too. The army, on the other hand, did not permit enrollees in its college ROTCs to play football. However, the army changed its mind on ROTC playing rules the following year, in 1944. The NCAA also allowed players who could not compete as freshmen to have one more year of eligibility.

Five of the top 10 teams in the final Associated Press Poll of 1943 were attached to naval training operations: Iowa Pre-Flight, the Naval Academy, Great Lakes, Del Monte Pre-Flight, and March Field. Notre Dame won the national title, and Michigan, which was in the navy program, finished third. Ohio State, however, had chosen to go Army, and it ended up nowhere. Brown was forced to play 17-year-olds because as soon as they reached their next birthday, unless they had an exemption, they had to enter the military. This, by itself, was a frustration. Brown's coaching philosophy was based on gradually introducing players into his system before they became regulars. There was no chance to do that now. They had to be force-fed.

So the 1942 "Scarlet Scourge" had turned into the 1943 "Baby Bucks."

Brown was furious. He knew that no blame would attach to him, but that didn't soothe his sense of injustice at what was happening to his underaged players.

"Not only were we being unfair to a group of 17-year-old kids," he said, "but we were exposing them to serious injury. Some of my players were taking a terrible beating from the older, more experienced athletes they faced."

On one level he understood that it was important to save the continuity of the Ohio State program. But on the other he wondered if the university really understood what it was asking of these players. For the first time, he began to question whether he belonged in Columbus.

The Buckeyes opened the 1943 season against the same team that had closed their championship run. But this Ohio State squad was no match for Iowa Pre-Flight. Everything that Brown had feared came true, and the Seahawks romped over their opponents, 28–13.

His team dispatched a similarly undermanned University of Missouri outfit, though, and fought hard against another of the great naval base teams, Great Lakes, before going down 13–6.

But then reality set in. The Buckeyes were throttled in succession by Purdue University, Northwestern University, and Indiana University. Brown's team was reeling from four losses in a row, looking up at 1–5 with no hope for the rest of the season.

Ohio State did manage to play one of the strangest games in its history before running out the string. The University of Illinois game, apparently, had ended in a 26–26 tie. The teams left the field, the crowd filed out of Ohio Stadium, the officials trotted to their locker room. But an employee of The Columbus Dispatch, who had been working the sidelines, noticed something that everyone else had missed. On Ohio State's final play, an official had dropped a penalty flag. The newsman knew the rules. A game cannot end with a penalty on the defense. He ran to speak with the officials to check on what the call had been.

It was confirmed that the penalty was an off-side against Illinois. But the official who made the call had watched everyone leave the field and decided he'd just quietly pick up the flag. That couldn't be allowed to stand. The head of the officiating crew ran to the two locker rooms to inform the coaches what had happened.

With the decision in his lap, Brown decided he had nothing to lose. He told his team to go back on the field and line up for a field goal.

He later admitted that two things had not occurred to him. His young kicker, John Stungis, had never tried a field goal in college. And if Illinois blocked the kick, the Illini could conceivably run it back for a touchdown and win the game.

Most of the crowd had already gone home, believing it had seen a tie. A few spectators were making their way across the back of the end zone where the kick would be tried. They stopped in confusion when they saw the players running back onto the field, still pulling on their equipment.

Illinois coach Ray Eliot was bitterly complaining that the game was over when the officials declared it was over. There was no precedent in the rules for allowing this to happen.

Brown sized up the scene and thought the spectators standing behind the end zone might help because they made the distance for the kick appear shorter than it actually was.

Stungis made the field goal, and OSU had one of the most improbable wins in its history; equaled in college football, perhaps, only by the Stanford-California game in which the winning touchdown was scored by running a kickoff through the marching band.

But the next week was the game that really stung. After a tie and a loss, Michigan coach Fritz Crisler was in no mood to hold back. His Wolverines manhandled the Buckeyes, 45–7, before just 39,000 spectators; the smallest crowd to watch this game in Ann Arbor since 1919.

Brown felt that his coaching opponent was rubbing it in. After the previous year's victory, Brown had saluted him graciously by saying "It would suit me if I could grow to be like Crisler. He's high class."

Crisler had responded by saying he had lost to "a great football team and a beautiful coach."

No sweet words this time around. When Crisler was lifted in triumph by his players, Brown said that he wouldn't care to be carried off the field for beating a team of 17-year-olds.

Rubbing it in whenever possible would become a standard practice in this bitter rivalry. Crisler's 1946 team defeated the Buckeyes 58–6. During his regime, Woody Hayes twice ran up 50 points on the Wolverines. The second occasion, in 1968, caused such a furor in Ann Arbor that it led directly to the hiring of Bo Schembechler as Michigan's coach. (It was Brown who would recommend Hayes for the head coaching job at his own alma mater, Miami University, a post that led directly to Ohio State and two national championships.)

Brown was now 35 years old, and he was informed that as a "person of prominence" he could expect to be inducted into the service. A few months after the season ended he joined the navy as a lieutenant, junior grade, with the assignment to coach the football team at Great Lakes Naval Training Base near Chicago. It would be the first time since leaving Severn School that he would coach a team outside Ohio. It would also be the last time.

The experience of 1943 had left a sour taste in his mouth. While he intended to return to Ohio State after the war, he also decided to remain open to other opportunities. At Great Lakes he would be coaching college graduates who might otherwise be playing professionally. Who knew where that could lead?

Brown's longtime assistant, Carroll Widdoes, was placed in charge of the Ohio State program after Brown's departure. Les Horvath, who was in dental school, returned to the team. He ended up winning the Heisman Trophy—the only time it has ever gone to someone who had not played the previous season.

The reinvigorated Buckeyes swept to an undefeated season and trailed only Army in the final poll. But by then Brown was at Great Lakes and could only cheer from afar.

Great Lakes had a distinguished football history, going back to World War I. Its 1918 team had been undefeated, held George Gipp's Notre Dame squad to a 7–7 tie, and ended up winning the Rose Bowl against California's Mare Island Marines.

Tony Hinkle had coached Great Lakes in 1943 and finished 10–2, defeating Notre Dame in the season's final game to spoil a perfect record for the Irish. Hinkle's team finished sixth in the national polls.

Hinkle was the longtime basketball coach at Butler University. He led Great Lakes to the service championship in that sport, in addition to continuing the football tradition. His Bluejackets were 18–5–1 in the two years before Brown arrived.

The Great Lakes baseball team was also a stellar group, led by another outstanding sports figure from Ohio, Bob Feller.

For most of the athletes at Great Lakes this was a way station. Base commanders liked to have winning teams for purposes of morale and their own egos. Great Lakes was no exception. When sports stars entered the service, the base commander made sure that as many as possible came to Great Lakes before taking up regular military duties. They would, eventually, be sent on to the war, though. If a player violated the rules, he could be sent out immediately—a responsibility that weighed heavily on Brown.

His usual strict regimen—no drinking, no smoking, no women—was unenforceable in this setting. These were mature men he was coaching, not schoolboys. They knew that in a few more months they could be facing imminent death. With that in mind, taking a drink did not seem like such a terrible infraction.

Brown had coached in a military-like environment before. But this was the real thing. He wore a sidearm, and as an officer, he was assigned regular responsibilities in conducting military drills. Coaching came second.

Hinkle, his predecessor, was already on active duty in the South Pacific. That prospect also hung over Brown as the 1944 season began, even though the war seemed to be winding down that autumn. The Allies were racing across Belgium and battling their way up the Italian peninsula. Paris and Rome had been liberated. Germany was in their sights. But the vicious island-hopping campaign was still going on in the Pacific. Another amphibious landing had been made at Peleliu, in the Palau Islands, one day before Great Lakes kicked off the start of the new season. Halfway around the world the greater battle was still raging. The thinking was that the war in the Pacific still had a long way to go. Inevitably, there would be a bloody invasion of the Japanese home islands late in the following year or in 1946. That's what life after football seemed to hold for both Brown and the men he coached.

But before the men faced active duty, they had football games to win. Hinkle had installed a simplified version of the Chicago Bears offense, and Brown had no choice but to implement it when he took over. It was too late to change it in favor of his own style of offense. He was so unaccustomed to the alternate formations that he even had to write down the numbering system for the plays on a sheet of paper as he stood on the sidelines.

Besides having to contend with a foreign style of offense and college programs revived by the new army rules on ROTC enrollees, the NCAA regulations for 1944 also disqualified professional athletes from service teams. So Brown was working with a much weaker hand.

Still, he had some talented players from Notre Dame and Iowa Pre-Flight; a big defensive end from Georgia in George Young, and a young halfback enrolled at Miami who quickly impressed Brown with his intelligence. His name was Ara Parseghian.

Brown was able to guide this group to four wins and a tie before running into his old friends from Ohio State. He said later that this game, which he lost 26-6, was an especially difficult experience, leaving him with "an empty feeling." He was facing his longtime friend and assistant, Widdoes, and the players he had personally recruited and coached.

Brown felt no particular attachment to the team he had taken over at Great Lakes. Many of them, he knew, were playing only to put off active duty. They accepted winning and losing with equal diffidence. It was not the sort of football Brown wanted to coach. It was only a tour of duty, like any other in time of war.

There were five more wins in a row. Only one of them came against a team with a winning record, however, and that was a defeat of Fort Warren.

A strong Notre Dame team brought Great Lakes back to reality with a sharp 28-7 slapdown in the season finale. Still, the team had finished 9-2-1, good enough to be within the top 20 in the Associated Press Poll.

Brown would be around again for the 1945 season, and he felt much better about those prospects. He knew the routine, had familiarized himself with the navy's way of doing things, saw some promise in the talent coming to Great Lakes, and had a chance to introduce some rudiments of his system to the players. But before a single game was played that fall, everything had changed—for the country and for Brown.

It began as an announcement on the country's sports pages over the 1944 Labor Day weekend. The *Chicago Tribune* bannered it across the top because the idea was the brainstorm of its sports editor, Arch Ward.

There was to be a new eight-team professional football league, the All-America Football Conference. New teams in New York and Chicago would go head-to-head with existing teams in the National Football League already based in those cities. There would be others in Buffalo, Miami, and Brooklyn. There would even be two franchises out in California. And one in Cleveland.

A journalist who got involved in such a promotion today would be fired before the story ever saw print. But those were different times and different customs. Ward had been the idea man behind baseball's All-Star Game, which is still going strong. He had come up with the plan for a football All-Star Game, too, played each August at Chicago's Soldier Field, matching the previous year's NFL champions against a team of graduating college stars. That game, eventually, was discontinued when pro coaches complained that it delayed high draft choices from learning their systems. It also was too embarrassing when the collegians won.

But this new league was going a step beyond a news promotion. Ward was also getting involved in organizing it and bringing in investors. Still, the *Tribune* accepted it.

The economic rationale was simple. The NFL was a struggling enterprise. There were solid franchises in the Chicago Bears, Green Bay Packers, New York Giants, and Washington Redskins. These teams had won every championship but one since the 1933 season, which is usually regarded as the date when the league's structure took its present form.

The other teams, however, were not so hot. The Pittsburgh Steelers had to combine with the Philadelphia Eagles to field a team in 1943, and with the Chicago Cardinals for 1944. Even the two of them together would not win a game in the upcoming season. The Cleveland Rams suspended operations entirely in 1943. There were nearly insolvent franchises in Boston and Brooklyn. Philadelphia and Detroit were treading water.

College football got the headlines. Interest in the professional game was limited to a coterie of fans in a small circle of cities.

Ward and others, however, anticipated an unprecedented boom in sports after the war ended. There was certainly a pent-up demand. Since the 1920s, when sports first became big business in America, the country had been through the Great Depression and war. Surely, when peace finally came, one hell of a party was going to bust loose. Americans would be looking for some fun, and those who supplied it stood to get rich.

Besides, many of the biggest stadiums in the country were not affiliated with the NFL. Yankee Stadium, the Los Angeles Coliseum, Soldier Field, Kezar Stadium in San Francisco, the Orange Bowl in Miami—they would all be available for teams from a new league.

This sort of thinking wasn't limited to football. The same set of conditions would lead to the Basketball Association of America, the forerunner of the National Basketball Association starting play in 1946. Boxing promoters already were drooling over the prospects of a Joe

Louis–Billy Conn rematch. Just as soon as they could get this damn war over with.

Ward's group had been meeting for three months before the formal announcement. He had assembled an impressive bunch of big money backers in trucking, oil, and lumber. He also had some big names who said they wanted in on the deal, including former heavyweight champ Gene Tunney, movie star Don Ameche, and Mrs. Lou Gehrig. One of the most enthusiastic supporters was Arthur McBride. He had made a fortune in the newspaper circulation business in Chicago, Florida real estate investments, and the biggest taxicab company in Cleveland, where he now lived. His sons attended Notre Dame, and whenever the Irish were at home, McBride made the trip to South Bend, Indiana. He idolized Frank Leahy, who had coached Notre Dame to the Associated Press title in 1943.

Its organizers insisted that the AAFC would play strictly by the rules. It would not try to raid the NFL, but it would sign players coming out of the military and colleges instead. It announced that some college stars already were under contract: Bob Daley from Minnesota and Iowa Pre-Flight, Glenn Dobbs of the University of Tulsa, and quarterback Angelo Bertelli of Notre Dame's title team.

The new league had its doubters right from the get-go. Chicago had one struggling franchise in the Cardinals, and already there were rumors about a deal in the works to send them out to Los Angeles. How could Chicago possibly support another team? Same thing with the weak NFL team in Brooklyn. How could a third New York team do any better? Cleveland had given the Rams lukewarm support. Why did anyone think a brand new team there would be any more successful?

The new league named Jim Crowley as its commissioner. His old teammate on Notre Dame's Four Horsemen, Elmer Layden, held the same job with the NFL. When asked about the new league, Layden laughed: "Let them get a ball first."

But he misjudged the seriousness of this threat to the NFL. There had been a few brief attempts to start rival leagues, but they all were underfinanced and folded quickly. This league meant business. It even signed a charter contract with United Airlines, the biggest such deal in aviation history, to fly its teams across the country. The NFL took the train.

McBride was after the biggest name of all. He wanted Leahy to coach his team. Only a personal appeal from the university's president dissuaded McBride.

Then he settled on Brown.

McBride had contacts on Cleveland's newspapers and had asked *The Plain Dealer*'s John Dietrich, who covered Ohio State, for a recommendation. Dietrich said it should be Brown. McBride said later that he'd never heard of him. He wasn't a big football fan, he just loved Notre Dame.

It was actually Ward who made the initial approach. Brown was in the navy for the duration of the war, still preparing to coach Great Lakes in the 1945 season, still expecting that he would be sent overseas. But he also had promised himself that he would listen if other opportunities came knocking. This one showed up with chimes.

Brown was offered $17,500 a year, more than any football coach at any level was being paid and almost two and a half times what he would be making at Ohio State. He was also offered a percentage of team ownership and a monthly stipend for the rest of his time in the navy.

In addition to all that, Brown was feeling like the soldier who had just learned that his old sweetheart was sitting under the apple tree with someone else. The game against Ohio State had taken a severe emotional toll. When the Buckeyes swept on to a perfect season and Widdoes was named Coach of the Year, Brown was left with a deeply conflicted state of mind.

That was his team. He had assembled it, put its parts together. But how could he go back to Columbus now and reclaim his old job from Widdoes after such an accomplishment? He was assured that the head coaching position would be his. But it seemed to him that the university's statements were formal and based on contractual necessities.

"I needed more than that," he wrote later. "I needed to be pampered a bit and told I truly would be welcomed."

This was an odd reaction from a man who had been hailed as the greatest hero in Ohio less than two years before. But a lot had happened since then. Maybe too much.

On February 9, 1945, it was announced that Brown had accepted McBride's offer and would coach the Cleveland team in the AAFC as soon as play began. The news made front-page headlines across Ohio, and Ward also plastered it across the top of his bailiwick at the *Tribune*. "A Brilliant Addition to All-America's List," read the line above a photo of Brown in his navy uniform, signing the five-year deal in Chicago.

"I leave Ohio State reluctantly," he said. "But it was time to decide whether to continue as a professor or a businessman. I couldn't turn down this deal in fairness to my family."

McBride said that nothing would be done without Brown's approval while he remained at Great Lakes.

"You know me," Brown added. "I'm going to try and build a dynasty."

The reaction at Ohio State was immediate and furious. Most fans sided with Brown, feeling that the university's administration had blown it. Widdoes was a different kind of personality. He did not want the spotlight. He wasn't comfortable with the media or the boosters. He enjoyed being an assistant coach, and he fully understood the pressures that came with the top job at Ohio State. The alumni did not see in him the dynamo they so admired in Brown. Even an undefeated season hadn't changed that.

But no one had said that to Brown. Or if they had, he wasn't listening.

Widdoes would go on to a 7–2 record in 1945 (losing to Michigan) and then resign the head coaching job, trading places with backfield coach Ray Bixler. Widdoes wanted no part of running the show anymore, even after compiling the greatest winning percentage in Ohio State's history.

Brown went back to preparing for the 1945 season at Great Lakes, but with a new sense of purpose. He would use it as a laboratory, a place to test out some theories before coaching his first professional game.

∽ · ∽

But he was in for an unpleasant surprise when he went back to work at Great Lakes. The influx of star players he was expecting for the 1945 season wasn't coming.

Base commanders on the West Coast argued that Great Lakes would be phased out soon, as soon as the war in Europe ended. The Pacific theater was where the navy's priorities were going to be, they said. They managed to get transfers to California for almost all the big-name college players. Great Lakes was left with the rest.

One familiar face did turn up, though, a former opponent from Canton McKinley High School. Marion Motley had gone on to play at South Carolina State University and the University of Nevada. Those schools were simply too small to come to the attention of the West Coast glory grabbers. Besides, he was black, and in 1945 that was also a strong consideration.

But at 230 pounds Motley was bigger than most interior linemen, and he could run like a halfback. Best of all, he loved to block.

Brown had used the single-wing formation in high school and college. But he recognized the possibilities of the T formation as soon as he saw it used against him by Missouri. It was the system he had inherited from Hinkle at Great Lakes, and he already was committed to using it in Cleveland.

With Motley, he saw the perfect vehicle for making it work.

Brown always had a fondness for fullbacks to keep defenses honest, from Bob Glass on his first championship team at Massillon Washington High School to Gene Fekete at Ohio State. But Motley was bigger and faster than either one of them.

The trap play had been used for years in the single-wing system as a way of slowing down the charge of overeager defensive linemen. But what if it were modified to be run out of a passing formation? Then the passes would be used to set up the run. A fullback who seemingly had been kept in the backfield to pass block could take a delayed handoff and face only smaller linebackers once he got past the line of scrimmage.

Brown was intrigued by the possibility. The only hitch was he needed to develop an effective quarterback to give the passing attack credibility. This was difficult at Great Lakes because, as the season began, his personnel were constantly being shuttled in and out.

Before a single play was run in the new season, though, the war ended in an atomic cloud. Japan surrendered in August, and the formal documents were signed aboard the battleship USS *Missouri* in early September.

Some athletes already were coming home. Hank Greenberg and Virgil Trucks returned in time to lead the Detroit Tigers to the World Series crown. Chicago Cubs catcher Clyde McCullough was, in fact, given a special waiver, and he remains the only man ever to play in the Series without appearing in a single regular-season game. But those were rarities. Even though the war was over, America remained a nation in arms. It would take several more months before most of the troops were demobilized and peace truly returned.

The practical effect of the end of hostilities, though, was that several of the stars who had been grabbed away from Great Lakes were now returned to Brown. Among them were three former Notre Dame players: quarterback George Terlep, linebacker Marty Wendell, and end Bucky O'Connor. Brown also found a fine running back in Frank Aschenbrenner, who would go on to play for Northwestern.

The Great Lakes Bluejackets started the season 0-4-1 before these reinforcements arrived and could be fit into the system. The team had managed to score only 20 points in these five games and had been shut out twice. Then it all clicked in. They reeled off five straight wins, and then for the fourth consecutive season, Great Lakes prepared to close its season against Notre Dame.

There was a sea of emotion surrounding this game. Not only would it end the season, in all probability it would be the last game ever played between these teams, definitely the last ever played at the Great Lakes stadium, which would be torn down shortly after the game's conclusion. Since the brief series had begun in 1942, the teams were 1-1-1. The outcome of this game would decide the ultimate winner.

Above all, this was Notre Dame, representing the pinnacle of college football. The Irish had been beaten up twice by Army in 1944 and 1945, by scores of 59–0 and 48–0. But those games were recognized as aberrations. Army was a vastly superior team during the war years, an all-star squad made up of outstanding players from colleges around the country. Aside from that one loss, Notre Dame had swept through its schedule in 1945 and fought the highly regarded Navy team to a tie. The following year it would win the national championship.

The Irish had ripped through Great Lakes the previous year. Brown knew that with the assignment in Cleveland on the horizon, this probably would be his last chance ever to coach against Notre Dame.

All in all, there was a heroic twilight about this early December game. Brown closed his practices, ringing the field with shore patrol. He knew that wherever Notre Dame played, even at Ohio State, there was a huge number of fans who would support them over the nominal home team. He was taking no chances on sympathetic sailors spilling the beans at Great Lakes.

"He was always strung tight," said his 1935 captain at Massillon, Augie Morningstar. "The closer to the game, the more sober he was until he was sure he had taken care of all the technical aspects."

That's how he operated throughout his career, and the final game at Great Lakes was no exception. At last, he felt that this was his team, not a bunch of strangers who were just passing through. And he badly wanted them to beat Notre Dame.

Motley was even eligible for discharge before the game was played. But he refused to leave.

The game has largely faded from memory. Great Lakes did not have the sort of alumni who keep such stories alive for generations, and the Irish were not eager to recapitulate the details. Great Lakes dismantled them, 39–7, in what was the last wartime college game.

Notre Dame led briefly, 7–6, in the first quarter. Then Aschenbrenner and Motley went to work. Brown realized what a force Motley was, as Terlep's passes began loosening up the Notre Dame defense. The trap play Brown had been developing all season was unleashed, and Motley ran over and through the smaller defenders trying vainly to stop him.

In another year, this would become part of the basic arsenal of the Cleveland attack. Brown called it the draw play.

Within weeks of this final game he received his discharge. His military career was over, and he was on his way home to Ohio. The transformation from local hero to national legend was about to begin.

8

1946: Cleveland Browns 14, New York Yankees 9

The Cleveland, Ohio, that Paul Brown returned to from the navy in 1946 was a booming, confident city. Its industries had played a major role in the war effort and the prosperity they brought in was evident everywhere. It could be seen in the department stores, filled with consumer goods again, along Euclid Avenue, and in the crowds of office workers along the Mall. There were out-of-town salesmen in the bustling hotel lobbies at the Hotel Cleveland on Public Square and the Hotel Hollenden on Superior Avenue. And the return of a strong industry was evidenced by the belching smokestacks along the Cuyahoga River.

It was the sixth-biggest city in the United States, trailing only New York and Chicago for the number of corporate headquarters. Paint, steel, auto parts, paper—that's what they made there.

Cleveland had been the model for Sinclair Lewis's satirical portrait of American boosterism, *Babbitt*, but it was also where Henry Luce chose to start up his experimental newsmagazine, *Time*. The Rockefeller fortune was built there, and along with other civic-minded millionaires, the Rockefellers had given the city an incomparable collection of museums and parks. Cleveland was wide awake, a city on the move.

Also on the move were the Cleveland Rams, the city's franchise in the NFL since 1937. Almost as soon as Brown was announced as the coach apparent of the AAFC team, early in 1944, Rams owner Dan Reeves began planning his exit.

The Rams had been a flimsy enterprise from the start. It originated as part of the old American Football League, which had collapsed in a swamp of bad debts. Owner Horace Marshman transferred the Cleveland franchise to the NFL, although with an entirely new roster. It was called the Rams after the Fordham University teams because that was the favorite school of general manager Buzz Wetzel.

Marshman tried playing in the mammoth Lakefront Stadium, but the crowds were not too eager to watch his 1–10 team compete. So in 1938 the Rams took their home games to the other extreme, the playing field at Shaw High School. They fired the coach, improved slightly to 4–7, and Marshman was emboldened to return to the lakefront.

He hired Dutch Clark, a tailback who had fired the Detroit Lions to the 1935 championship, as his coach. But that didn't help much, and in 1941 Marshman sold the team to two local businessmen, Reeves and Fred Levy Jr. They immediately moved it again, out of the cavernous downtown stadium and into the much smaller League Park. That's where baseball's Indians played most of their home games, over on the east side of town.

Things got even dicier in 1943. Both Reeves and Levy had to leave for military service, and the Rams decided to suspend operations. There was little evidence that Cleveland missed them. Before departing, though, Reeves bought out Levy's interest in the team, and that turned out to be the most significant development in the history of the Rams.

They drafted UCLA quarterback Bob Waterfield in 1944. When he joined them the following year, the reversal of fortune was immediate. The team went 9–1, Waterfield was named the league's Most Valuable Player by unanimous vote (the first time that ever happened), and a smattering of fans began finding their way to the Lakefront, where the team once again was playing.

In December they beat the Washington Redskins, 15–14, on a frozen field with the wind howling in from Lake Erie. Cleveland was the champion of the football world.

One month after this triumph, Reeves told the city he was outta there. He had looked over the terrain, knew that he would be bucking a rival coached by the greatest football hero in Ohio, and saw the glimmer of California gold. He was taking the Rams to Los Angeles.

The NFL fought the move. Even though the AAFC already had promised to put two teams on the West Coast, it was still regarded as much too distant. For instance, Major League Baseball's westernmost outpost was St. Louis. Did Reeves know something baseball didn't?

Reeves had to threaten to take his franchise out of the NFL and agree to underwrite travel expenses for visiting teams before the league would let him go.

When it finally did, Gordon Cobbledick, *The Plain Dealer*'s sports columnist, cheerfully waved good-bye.

"The Rams made no attempt to market themselves to the fans," he wrote. "They never fully recovered from the decision not to field a team in 1943."

Reeves turned out to be one of the game's great innovators. Capitalizing on Waterfield's local reputation at UCLA, he built the Rams into a glamour team, with a wide-open offense that packed the Coliseum. Reeves was among the first to recognize the potential of television, and he put his team on the tube as soon as possible. He was among the first to employ a full-time scouting staff. After some initial financial losses, Reeves eventually put the rival AAFC franchise out of business. The move west had paid off handsomely.

The new Cleveland team was doing just fine, too. And it was now officially called the Browns.

A contest was held in May 1945 to pick a name, with the prize for the winning entry being a $1,000 war bond. *The Plain Dealer* cautioned contestants: "Don't suggest Cleveland Browns. Only about 75,000 other people will think of the same thing!"

The winner was Cleveland Panthers, but it soon was pointed out that a semipro team from the 1920s had also used that name. When he heard that, Brown rejected it.

"I won't stand for anything that smacks of failure," he said from his office at Great Lakes. "That old Panthers team failed. I want no part of that name."

Despite *The Plain Dealer*'s warning, a majority of entries had favored the Cleveland Browns. So the team surrendered to the popular will and announced on August 14, 1945, that Browns it would be. It was an unmistakable measure of the coach's stature in this city and another clear reason for Reeves to bolt.

Brown professed to be uncomfortable with the decision. For years afterward he argued that the real origin of the name was to honor heavyweight champ Joe Louis, the "Brown Bomber." Why a Cleveland team would name itself for a fighter who called Detroit his home was a bit of a mystery. But that was Brown's story.

There was no confusion, however, over what he was setting out to do. He made that absolutely clear.

"You don't win with dogs," he said. "I will select my players on the basis of personality, as well as ability. For a coach to succeed he first has to mold his players so that the fit will be his own.

"I will ask the same of these players as I did at Ohio State. The difference is that they will draw a salary, and we will provide them with business opportunities. But I may select the most amateur team in pro football because I want players with a love for the game."

He also made no secret of the fact that he had a marked preference for Ohio people and for veterans "because they are known quantities."

Brown already had said that he intended to "build a dynasty," and he meant it. "I want to be what the New York Yankees are in baseball or Ben Hogan is in golf."

When the word *dynasty* was used in connection with professional football in 1946, the only possible benchmark was the Chicago Bears. They were the closest thing to a dynasty the league ever had seen. Since the NFL adopted its current structure, only one team ever had repeated as champions up to that time—the 1940–41 Bears.

The Bears' owner-coach George Halas had hired Clark Shaughnessy to come over from the University of Chicago when that school gave up playing football in 1938, and to bring along his theories about running the T formation.

No one yet had tried this offense in the pros. Brown introduced to it memorably in his first game at Ohio State University, in 1941, when the University of Missouri's Don Faurot sprang it on him. Shaughnessy would go on to win the Rose Bowl out of the T formation as the head coach at Stanford University.

But it was the Bears who made it an unstoppable weapon. Halas had scoured the college ranks to find the player who could best fit the new system. He came up with the name of Columbia University tailback Sid Luckman and traded up in the draft to get him. Luckman had played in the single wing, but Shaughnessy was sure he could run the T.

Shaughnessy worked with Luckman intensively for two years. When Luckman and the Bears sprang the complete package on Washington in the 1940 championship game, they won 73–0. From then on, the T was recognized as the future of football.

Even Redskins quarterback Sammy Baugh, regarded as the greatest single-wing passer of his day, made the switch. He then turned it against the Bears and took the 1942 title from them—the only thing that prevented Chicago from winning four championships in a row.

The Bears had shown what offensive innovation and careful selection of the right players could accomplish. Brown saw no reason why he couldn't follow that route. In fact, he knew the man who could take him there. He already had beaten Brown twice.

Otto Graham entered Northwestern University as a basketball player and music major. Both his parents were musicians, and while attending high school in Waukegan, Illinois, he had won a state-wide competition on the French horn. He was also a better-than-competent violinist. But when football coach Pappy Waldorf saw him throw passes in an intramural game, he persuaded Graham to give his sport a try.

Graham wound up a first-team All-American in basketball as a college senior and finished third in the Heisman balloting in football. He also found time to letter in baseball.

Brown first got a look at him in 1941. With Graham at tailback, the Wildcats gave Ohio State its only defeat of the season. He did it again to Brown's Baby Bucks two years later. He did it to a lot of teams. By the time he graduated, Graham held the Big Ten record for passing yardage. He was even fast enough to be used on punt returns, an unheard-of assignment for any contemporary quarterback.

Graham entered the U.S. Navy Air Corps after graduation, and it was there that Brown sought him out. He didn't have to go far. Graham was stationed just a few miles from Great Lakes, at the Glenview, Illinois, Naval Air Station. Brown offered him a contract of $7,500 a year and a monthly payment of $250, a princely stipend for the time, for the duration of the war.

"All I asked was, where do I sign?" Graham said. "Some of the other navy men said I was rooting for the war to last forever."

Graham had been drafted by the Detroit Lions. It was assumed by the NFL that the players it had drafted and those who had gone into the military would return to their teams after the war. But that was a false assumption. The draft choices were unsigned, and the contracts of most military veterans had expired. The AAFC said it would not raid NFL teams. But it did not regard signing players who were not under contract as a raid. Nor did it shy away from signing NFL players who decided to go with the new league of their own volition. Bears tackle Lee Artoe was the first to do exactly that, and the older league knew it was in for a fight.

When Graham's signing was announced on March 31, 1945, it touched off a full-scale salary war. By football's 1946 All-Star Game, 44 of the 60 collegiate players had signed with the AAFC. Just so everyone knew that, Ward, the journalistic promoter whose newspaper sponsored the game, wrote adulatory features on those who had chosen to pass up the NFL.

Pat Harder, the former University of Wisconsin star who went on to a long career in the NFL, said the situation was so one-sided that "I even doubted that I would get to play."

The San Francisco 49ers announced the signing of Stanford's great T-formation wizard, Frankie Albert, as well as his teammate from the 1943 Rose Bowl champs, running back Norm Standlee. Chicago picked up Elroy Hirsch (who had yet to be known as "Crazylegs") and former Indiana University running back Bob Hoernschemeyer. The New York franchise, always critical to the success of any league in any sport, signed Ace Parker and the former Detroit Lions star and league MVP, Frank Sinkwich.

Most of the teams went after the biggest names available, in a helter-skelter manner. But Brown was a man with a plan.

Graham was the cornerstone, but all through 1945 and early 1946, Brown continued building his team. John Brickels was his point man. A former high school football coach in Ohio, Brickels went on to coach basketball at the University of West Virginia, taking the Mountaineers into the 1945 National Invitational Tournament. But when Brown offered him a position with Cleveland, he jumped at it.

Brickels was a glib, persuasive man, and he also knew the Ohio territory. That, in Brown's mind, was essential. Working out of a small office in downtown Cleveland, Brickels paid visits to the players Brown wanted.

Helping with the legal details was Creighton Miller, a former Notre Dame player who also happened to be the nephew of the mayor of Cleveland. This was before the Rams had announced their departure, and owner McBride, who stayed mostly in the background, was making sure all the political bases were covered for his team.

By the summer of 1945, Brown's old boys were coming aboard in droves. Brickels signed Gene Fekete, the fullback on the Ohio State championship team of three years prior. He also got the signature of Lin Houston, who had been on Brown's A-list since he was in junior high at Massillon Washington High School. The nimble guard, who also had played for Brown at Columbus, was being courted by several teams. But the same monthly payment given to Graham sealed Houston's signing with Cleveland, which was where he wanted to go anyhow.

Then there was George Cheroke, a 195-pound guard who had played for Brown at Ohio State and was the team's Sophomore of the Year in 1941. Another of Brown's former Buckeyes, tackle Jim Daniell, signed up, too.

Other signings did not go as smoothly. It seemed to Brown's former assistant, Carroll Widdoes, who was still the head coach at Ohio State, that Brown was targeting the Buckeyes; persuading players coming out of the service to turn pro instead of returning to school. Widdoes was especially irate over Lou Groza and Dante Lavelli. Both had college eligibility left but chose Cleveland over Columbus.

Brown knew them well. He had recruited them for OSU, snatching both of them away from Notre Dame, and he knew they would fit right in with the team he was assembling. After all, they were both Ohio boys and veterans.

Groza had been an outstanding lineman at Martin's Ferry, and his tackle play alone would have commended him to the coach. But Brown could not help noticing that even as a high school player, his kickoffs were going 65 and 70 yards, without using a tee. That would always be useful.

Groza played just one season at Ohio State before going into the military. He was still serving in the South Pacific when he agreed to play for the Browns in May 1945. He went on the monthly installment plan and was also sent a football, so that he could practice his kicking in the Philippines.

Lavelli had been a quarterback at Hudson High School, outside Cleveland, but Brown convinced him to switch to end while he was on the Ohio State freshman team. He was injured early in the 1942 season and ended up playing only three games with the Buckeyes before he, too, had to enter the service. He said later that he went to his first professional game right after his discharge and decided on the spot that this was where he wanted to be. He was ready when Brown called.

Besides Widdoes, the Cleveland recruiting drive also teed off Papa Bear, George Halas.

The Bears had used a number-one pick to draft halfback Bob Steuber out of Missouri. Steuber actually played in the 1943 opener against Green Bay. But the next day he was called into the navy aviation cadet program at DePauw University. In one of the strangest twists of wartime college football, the NCAA ruled that Steuber still had a year of college eligibility left, even though he had already played as a pro.

This was good news for DePauw, which went on to destroy the other small college teams on its schedule. Halas could hardly wait to get him back in 1946.

But Brown remembered Steuber from the tough Missouri teams he had played at Ohio State and signed him up. To make matters worse, Brown brought in another former college opponent that he admired; halfback Edgar "Special Delivery" Jones, from the University of Pittsburgh. Jones had also been Bears property before the war.

Halas raged and threatened to sue. But the contracts had lapsed, and he had no case.

Brown did misstep, however, when he tried to sign center Vince Bannonis, only to find the Chicago Cardinals did hold a valid contract. Cleveland backed off immediately. But it didn't have to look very far for a replacement.

Several members of the Rams had decided they wanted to stay in Cleveland instead of moving out to Los Angeles. An examination of their contracts revealed they were, indeed, signed with the Cleveland Rams and not the Los Angeles Rams. That allowed Brown to bring in Mo Scarry as the starting center. It also gave Brown four other starters on the 1946 team: defensive tackles Ernie Blandin and Chet Adams and defensive backs Don Greenwood and Tom Colella, who handled the punting duties.

Brown went after yet another opposing player who had caught his eye. Great Lakes won its game against Fort Warren handily in 1945, but end Mac Speedie had impressed him. True, the fortuitously named receiver had grown up far from Ohio, way out in Utah, but Brown's offensive plan called for all the big pass catchers he could find, so he overlooked the geographic liability. Speedie was signed up.

Brickels sold Brown on two linemen from Marshall University whom he had seen during his time in West Virginia. Both Frank Gatski and Ed Ulinski also became longtime starters on the Browns.

The team was coming together nicely. But Brown had another agenda in mind, too.

Ever since his years at Massillon, his teams had been color blind. The best athletes played regardless of color, and there would be no backing down from that policy. But professional football had put up a color bar in 1933. Even though the league was situated almost entirely in the North (the Washington Redskins were the lone exception), it was a segregated entity through a "gentleman's agreement." Brown decided he would crack that barrier.

This was the summer of 1946. Jackie Robinson had yet to play an inning in the big leagues. That was still a year away. Brooklyn Dodgers general manager Branch Rickey had created a furor merely by signing him to a minor league contract and sending him to Montreal for this season. Long Island University star Dolly King would become the first black player to sign a professional basketball contract, with the Rochester Royals, in the fall.

Professional football had a history of employing black players almost from its beginning. They were present in the loosely organized leagues of the 20th century's first years, most notably in northeastern Ohio. Doc Baker was a running back for the Akron, Ohio, team in 1906. But the biggest name was Fritz Pollard, who not only excelled on the field but was Akron's coach in the Ohio League.

Pollard had grown up in Chicago, where he was an outstanding high school athlete. He was given a privately funded scholarship to Brown University and led the school to the Rose Bowl in 1916. He became the first African American to play in that game and to be named to an All-American team.

When he turned pro he was regarded as the league's biggest gate attraction, next to Canton's Jim Thorpe. After Akron joined the newly formed National Football League in 1922, Pollard remained as its top player and coach.

Other NFL teams did not shy away from signing black athletes either. Iowa had All-American tackle Duke Slater. Minnesota had end Rube Marshall. Rutgers had celebrated end Paul Robeson, who would soon ditch football for a career as a concert artist and actor. At least nine other black players also have been traced to NFL rosters in the 1920s by the African American Registry.

But as the Depression deepened, so did racial attitudes. Team owners claimed they were encountering resentment from their fans over employing black players when so many white people were without jobs. So the color bar went up.

The war changed a lot of things, however. Having seen the wider world, African Americans were becoming more assertive about claiming the rights they felt were owed to them as veterans. In the South, this led to a spike in lynchings and a revival of white-supremacist organizations. But in Northern cities some barriers were coming down. Brown felt that Cleveland was a place that would welcome this step.

Bill Willis had been a 202-pound tackle on Brown's 1942 team at Ohio State. Faster than most running backs (he ran the 60-yard and 100-yard dashes on the track team), his quickness was a disruptive force to anyone trying to come up the middle against the Buckeyes.

He had taken a year off between high school and college, and at age 22 Willis was the oldest member of the Baby Bucks of 1943. The following season he was voted to several All-American teams. Willis was chosen to play in the 1945 College All-Star Game—and with that his career seemed over. There were no jobs for him in the pros. He accepted the position as head coach at Kentucky State University, a black school. Still, he was just 24 years old, in peak physical condition, and he wanted to play.

Brown wanted him to play, too, but understood that he had to tread carefully. Through mutual friends he got word to Willis that if he showed up at the Browns' training camp at Bowling Green, Ohio, as a walk-on, he would get a tryout.

True to his word, Brown lined him up in a scrimmage opposite Scarry, the team's starting center. Willis ran over and around him on every play. On one snap, Willis had Scarry backing up so quickly that he stepped on Graham's foot before the quarterback could pull away.

Scarry was convinced that Willis had to be jumping offside. No one could possibly beat him so cleanly on every play. Brown got down on his hands and knees along the scrimmage line to make sure that Willis was not coming across too soon. He wasn't.

"I'd just been concentrating completely on the ball and the center's hands," he said. "At the slightest movement or tightening, I charged."

On that same day, Willis became one of the Browns.

There was one more critical position to fill. Brown needed a fullback, a man who could block and run with equal dexterity, to make his offensive scheme of passes and draw plays function. He had not forgotten his star at Great Lakes, the man who had destroyed Notre Dame with his unstoppable rushes up the middle. He went to find Marion Motley.

Like Willis, Motley was aware that football seemed to be a dead end. It was pointless to return to the University of Nevada to play out his eligibility. He was 26 years old and had a family to support. So he went home to Canton and got a job in the steel mill. That was to be his life from now on.

Again Brown did not feel he could invite Motley to Bowling Green directly. But he got word to him that if he wrote his former coach for a tryout, the door would be open. Motley wrote, and if the door had remained closed, Motley probably would have knocked it down.

In all fairness, it was Reeves who brought in the first black players that year for his Los Angeles team. A few weeks before Willis and Motley agreed to terms with Cleveland, Reeves had signed up former UCLA running back Kenny Washington and end Woody Strode (who went on to an acting career in the movies). Neither played as critical a role with the Rams, however, as the Cleveland players did with the Browns. But Los Angeles was first.

At this point in their careers, Motley outweighed Willis by some 30 pounds and was just as fast. There was no running back in the era who could match him for speed and power—and there wouldn't be until Jim Brown came along one decade later.

The AAFC did not require its players to go both ways, but Brown knew that with Motley he was not only getting a fullback but an outstanding outside linebacker as well. Motley started at both positions in his first two years with the Browns.

Brown later said that if Motley hadn't made the Hall of Fame as a fullback, he certainly would have been voted in as a linebacker.

Graham was delayed in getting his military discharge and didn't report to camp until late in the summer. Brown felt that Graham was not quite ready to start the opener. The coach didn't want any mishaps in the team's first game, so he turned instead to Cliff Lewis. Lewis was cast right in the Browns mold, a high school star in the

Cleveland suburb of Lakewood before going off to play college ball at Duke University.

Brown said that if there had been no Graham, Lewis could have been his starter. As it was, when Graham was deemed ready to play, Lewis switched to defense and started for the next four years at safety.

The first game in Cleveland Browns history was scheduled for the first Friday night in September 1946, at the Lakefront Stadium.

The coach was confident he had chosen well. At Massillon, Ohio State, Great Lakes—even at Severn School—he had inherited another coach's choices. But every spot on the Browns' roster was filled with a man he had hand-picked. There were no qualms about players who didn't fit in.

Still, there are always doubts. The entire AAFC was an unknown quantity. There was nothing yet to measure against.

But the city of Cleveland seemed convinced already. The crowd of 60,135 that showed up for the opener was the largest ever to attend a professional football game in any league. That mark would be exceeded twice during this season and four times in 1947.

As it turned out, Brown couldn't have asked for a better opponent. The Miami Seahawks turned out to be the weakest team in the league and ultimately an embarrassment. The Seahawks' absentee ownership was based in Atlanta and was severely underfunded. The coach, Jack Meagher, left Auburn University for this job. Like Brown, he favored regional talent. Tackle George Ellenson had been a Miami high school star, and running back Monk Gafford played for Meagher at Auburn.

But the team's light bankroll had lost most of the players it wanted to the NFL. Worse yet, owner Harvey Hester decided to play his home games on Monday night, when there would be no competition. He was on to something, as the later success of *Monday Night Football* would prove. But it turned out to be a disaster, literally, in south Florida.

According to longtime Atlanta sports columnist Furman Bisher, who covered this team, it rained during the first six home games. "On the seventh," he wrote, "there was a hurricane."

In addition, Miami was still a smallish city in 1946, with only 250,000 people in the entire metropolitan area. It was, by far, the smallest fan base in the league. The Seahawks would disappear in a hurricane of debt by the end of the season, with a 3–11 record, the worst in the AAFC.

The opener between the Seahawks and the Browns reflected all that. Lewis hit Speedie on a touchdown pass in the first quarter, and the rout was on. The Browns breezed to a 44–0 victory in their debut.

It wouldn't all be quite that easy. The team lost back-to-back games after a 7–0 start: to San Francisco, 34–20, before another record crowd at home, and then on the road in Los Angeles. But Graham, who had taken over as the starter in the third game, quickly got things righted. The Browns beat the 49ers in the rematch on the road, 14–7, and from then on the team was on a roll.

It won its final four games by scores of 51–14, 42–17, 34–0, and 66–14. Its overall record was 12–2, the best in the league's western division. Graham was the league's top-rated passer, and Motley rushed for an average carry of 8.2 yards. The Browns would go into the championship game at home against the New York Yankees.

The Yankees were no pushovers. They had finished the season at 10–3–1, although two of those losses had been to the Browns. The league's eastern division was much weaker than the west. Its bottom three teams had won only nine games combined, or one fewer than New York's total. But the Yankees had fought Cleveland to a tough 7–0 defeat in the mud in their regular-season meeting at New York before a packed Yankee Stadium. There was reason to suppose this could be a fairly equal match.

The Yankees' coach, Ray Flaherty, had won two championships with the Washington Redskins. Like Brown, he was a brilliant innovator. He had developed the screen pass as a devastating weapon for Baugh and employed two different offensive units in Washington, one for passing and one for rushing.

The biggest name signed by the Yankees, Sinkwich, turned out to be a bust. Some old knee injuries were aggravated while he was playing on a service team, and he couldn't move anymore. However, Spec Sanders, who had been a substitute at the University of Texas, ended up leading the league in rushing. And it turned out that tailback Parker, who had been the league MVP when he played for the NFL's Brooklyn Dodgers in 1940, had one more great season left in his arm.

Flaherty had put together a solid veteran team in New York, with recognizable names like Pug Manders and Bruiser Kinard in his lineup. He also had added a little spice to the contest by referring to the Browns as "a team from Podunk with a high school coach."

Flaherty had spent 20 years in the pro game as a player and coach, winning a championship with the Redskins while Brown was still at Massillon. While Flaherty's attitude played well in New York City (which regards everyplace else in the world as Podunk), it raised the annoyance level severely on Lake Erie.

Eleven years later, baseball's Yankees referred to Milwaukee's fans as "bush league" during a World Series because they held up signs to welcome the team train to their city. The Braves then beat them in the Series. Flaherty's remark turned out to be similarly unwise.

Flaherty thought he knew how to counter the Browns' T formation attack. He had put in a seven-man defensive front when the Yankees played San Francisco and managed to contain Frankie Albert. New York was also bigger than Cleveland, although many other coaches made the mistake of overemphasizing that factor when playing a Paul Brown team. Moreover, Parker had missed both games with the Browns during the regular season with injuries. He was ready to play in this one.

But ticket sales for the December 22 title game were disappointing. The big stadium was only half full, with the final crowd announced as 40,469, second smallest of the season. There had been a big snowstorm on the 20th, and a cold front had moved in. Besides, the Browns were two-touchdown favorites.

Thousands of fans who recalled the misery of sitting out in the ossifying freeze at the previous December's championship game with the

Rams decided to stay home this time and listen to Bob Neal and Stan Gee call the action on WGAR. It turned out to be a bitter defensive struggle and far more agonizing than the Browns fans had counted on.

The Yanks intercepted Graham in the first quarter and set up a field goal. It appeared that Cleveland then had gone ahead on a long pass play to Jones. But the officials ruled he had stepped out of bounds, and the drive fizzled when Graham was thrown for a loss on a fourth-down play at the New York 3.

Groza was playing on a sprained ankle, and Brown hesitated to use him in a situation that didn't seem to require a field-goal attempt. Groza's 13 three-pointers and 45 extra points during the season gave him the league's scoring title, but he would miss three field goals during the course of this afternoon.

Undeterred, Graham completed seven consecutive passes late in the second quarter and brought Cleveland down to the 13. Motley went the rest of the way on two straight runs, and the Browns led, 7–3.

But in the third quarter, Parker suddenly came to life and took the Yankees on an 80-yard march, half of it coming on three passes to end Jack Russell. Sanders went in from the 2-yard line. Although the extra point was blocked, New York entered the fourth quarter with a 9–7 lead.

Motley broke loose on a 51-yard run in the fourth quarter, but the hobbled Groza missed a field goal from the 12 that would have put Cleveland back ahead.

But legends are made at times like this. Staring straight at the upset, Graham began to move, completing a critical third-and-long pass to Jones and entering New York territory. Graham had thrown 17 touchdown passes during the season. Most of them went to Lavelli, who led the league in receiving yardage. Graham's 18th found Lavelli again. The end went up between two defenders in the end zone and pulled it in.

Cleveland led 14–9 with just five minutes to play. The Yankees weren't beaten, however, until a final Parker pass was intercepted. Who grabbed it? None other than Graham, who had entered the game as part of a prevent defense.

It had been a closely run game. By the slimmest of margins, and the grace of two Hall of Fame talents, the Browns legend escaped being tarnished before it had even begun.

But the high school coach from Podunk had conquered yet another football world on his very first try. And the Browns, who each went home $931.57 richer for their championship effort, had just gotten started.

9

1950: Cleveland Browns 35, Philadelphia Eagles 10

By any measure, this was the greatest era in the history of sports in Cleveland, Ohio.

The Indians would battle to the second World Series title in their history in 1948, shattering all baseball attendance records on the way. Lou Boudreau had been named manager of the Indians just weeks before Paul Brown was given the head coach's job at Ohio State University. Now Boudreau had finally ended the team's 28-year pennant drought and knocked off the Boston Braves in the Series.

That was hard for the Browns to top. But they did. After two consecutive AAFC championships, they went on to a third in 1948. But this time they finished with a perfect 15-0 record. It was a mark that wouldn't be surpassed until former Brown Don Shula led the Miami Dolphins to a 17-0 record in 1972.

How could it get any better than this?

Brown wasn't taking anything for granted, though. Success was always defined for him as a constant process of topping himself. He outlined his thoughts in a two-hour talk to his team before the 1947 season started. It was a ritual he would go through every year, with slight variations each time.

"Every season begins from scratch," he said. "Because football is a state of heart and mind, as well as physical. You must build on a broad foundation.

"If winning is worth something, it's worth everything.

"If you're cut from this team, be a man about it.

"Keep your wives out of football; it breeds trouble.

"We don't want thugs. I'll take my players high-class, cold, deadly, smart, hard-hitting, and hard-running.

"The worst thing you do to an opponent is to beat him.

"I don't want you to play for a paycheck. I want you to play for the sheer desire of licking somebody. If you're playing just for the money, leave right now.

"If you're a drinker or a chaser, you'll weaken the team. We don't want you. Don't smoke in public, and if you drink in public you're fired.

"Ten years from now, you'll be proud to say you played on this team."

He meant every word of it. The sure and swift punishment that came down when the rules were violated was part of team lore. Just before the 1946 AAFC title game, team captain Jim Daniell flunked a sobriety test when Cleveland police stopped his car. The story ran in the newspapers, and at a team meeting the next day, Brown asked the center if it were true. When he said it was, Brown told him to get out. Daniell was finished with the Browns.

This was Brown's starting center, one of the prized Ohio State boys. After that, Brown never had to invoke the rule against drinking again. The Browns understood that if he would throw Daniell off the team, no one would get special dispensation.

The system that would become part of the Paul Brown mystique was set in place.

Players were given graded tests on their playbooks and had to copy every play in a separate notebook. "If you copy it, you have a better chance to get it right," he said. Neatness counted. Cheating abounded on these tests, but Brown didn't care. The main thing was getting the material written down because some of it was bound to stick.

During road trips more review tests were given on the material. "I didn't want them to think they were on a pleasure trip," said Brown.

His players were also told to keep their elbows off the table when they ate and to refrain from sex after Tuesday nights during the season.

Brown would do his part to sacrifice by giving up his usual dry martini before dinner during the season.

His coaching staff was hired as full-time employees because he felt it was demeaning for them to be forced into taking off-season jobs to get by. The Browns always went first class, and that included mandatory coats and ties for the players on the road. Appearances counted.

He also paid special attention to his own grooming. "I was probably the first football coach to dress up," he said. His snap-brim hat and, when the cold came, his cashmere overcoat became trademarks. The knot in his necktie was always exposed and tight.

He retained his former advance man, John Brickels, as part of his permanent staff and also brought in defensive wizard Fritz Heisler, who had been on his staff at Massillon Washington High School and at Ohio State.

Brown invented the taxi squad during this time. He hated cutting a player who had put forth a good effort. ("Be a man about it.") Even worse than that, he hated the possibility of losing him to a competitor when a position could open up for him on the Browns because of injury.

Team owner Arthur McBride ran Cleveland's largest cab company. So Brown got jobs for these surplus players as drivers, where they could be called back to the active roster at a moment's notice. Hence, the taxi squad.

He continued to refine his practices. In fact, his first drill in training camp was a practice on how to practice. Every player and coach was assigned a specific task to work on at a given time, and they had better know what that was. He also began each practice, starting on Wednesdays each week, at 1:00 PM. That was the same time as the kickoff on Sundays. Brown understood how the body clock worked and wanted physical activity to peak at the right time. Practices lasted exactly one hour and 15 minutes because he believed that is as much activity as the mind can absorb and still be capable of learning. Eventually every other team in professional football adopted some form of these individual and team drills.

Brown applied the same theory of time management to himself. "I never believed in the stuff you read about coaches sleeping on cots in their offices and all that junk," he said. "What can you accomplish when you're mentally exhausted? Some of my best thinking comes in the morning after a good rest. All my life, I got to bed at a reasonable time."

The work ethic was the core of his being. But work without organization was wasted time, and he didn't believe in it. After all, his father's job was to make sure the trains ran on time, and that was a good lesson to absorb.

Another requirement of Brown's concerned the players' involvement with the press. "He didn't want us talking to reporters," recalled Edgar "Special Delivery" Jones, "and he didn't talk much to us."

Sometimes his players would have preferred he didn't talk at all. The Wednesday film sessions were dreaded by those who had fouled up the Sunday before. On one memorable occasion he kept rerunning the same sequence of center Mo Scarry missing a block. "Is that you, Mo?" he kept repeating to an utterly silent room. "Is that you?"

He never raised his voice, but the players singled out would cringe when Brown gave his standard summation: "Don't tell me the great ones do it that way."

Even Otto Graham was not immune. He was once the last man to arrive at one of these meetings. Although he was still on time, Brown took him aside afterward.

"Don't think your position is locked up," he told Graham. "You're supposed to be our leader. Earn your job."

When Marion Motley dozed off in the front row, Brown hit him in the face with a towel.

But through these constant film reviews and tests the Browns were never allowed to fall into bad habits. They were quickly and forcefully corrected.

The pregame routine was always the same. A movie and a hotel stay on the night before a game. The evening meal would be, recalled Graham, "dry steak, dry baked potato, dry salad. The stuff was so dry it'd choke you."

There would be no digestive problems when the Browns took the field.

Brown belonged to the Episcopal Church, and while he never displayed the overt religiosity of some contemporary football coaches, religion did provide his compass. Discipline, self-denial, hard work, order, respect for authority—with those values there was nothing you couldn't accomplish.

He had met Katy Kester in the 11th grade at Massillon, and there was never another girl for him. They were married the year before he graduated from college, in 1929. She understood his single-mindedness when it came to football and made her peace with it. Katy raised their three boys, cooked the meals, made sure he would come home to a house where things were managed as he liked them. She also understood the role of the coach's wife and played it perfectly, cheering at the right times and never giving away her concern when things were going badly. Brown used the word *serenity* to describe her presence, and she was his personal foundation.

The 1947 Browns were fairly much the same bunch that had won it all in their first year, with one seemingly minor addition. Weldon Humble was brought in to share the left-guard spot on the offensive line with Ed Ulinski and to start at linebacker. But the job description was much broader than that. The addition of Humble gave the team depth. Brown could now employ a system of messengers, sending in plays to Graham by alternating guards without losing any quality on the line.

The ridicule was immediate. Brown was accused of lacking respect for his quarterback, of reducing his players to puppets, of distorting the game.

"The quarterback is an important cog," he retorted. "But he is only a cog. From his place on the field he cannot possibly see how adjustments can be made so that a play can succeed."

That system now is just a matter of course, with coaches stationed high in the press box, communicating with the sidelines and sending in plays by phone. Some modern fans of the game may find it hard to believe this aspect of the game was once left entirely to a quarterback's discretion. But Brown was the first to understand how the unlimited substitution rule enabled him to coach more directly and effectively. By 1951 the system was instituted as full-time policy on the Browns.

The 1947 season was a virtual duplicate of the first. Cleveland even improved slightly, to 12-1-1. It lost only to the Los Angeles Dons and tied the Yankees in New York. On October 5, in the home game against New York, another record-breaking crowd of 80,067 packed the stadium to watch the Browns win 26-17.

The league's defunct Miami franchise had been transferred to Baltimore. Reflecting that area's interest in Thoroughbred racing, it was called the Colts. But there was big trouble in Chicago. After some initial curiosity, the noncontending AAFC team could not compete with either the Bears or the Cardinals for fan interest. The Bears won the NFL title in 1946, and the Cards, with the greatest team in their history, did the same in 1947.

When Cleveland went into Chicago to play the Rockets, only 18,000 spectators turned up at Soldier Field to watch the 41-21 drubbing. The team had no defense whatsoever and finished 1-13. It was the league's weak sister, but the AAFC felt it was essential to maintain a team there.

It came down to another Browns-Yankees title game. The Yanks again were a formidable opponent, with an 11-2-1 mark. The tie with the Browns after three straight losses even encouraged fans to believe that the Yankees were gaining on them.

Spec Sanders had rushed for 1,432 yards, the only man ever to top 1,000 in the history of the AAFC. With 19 touchdowns, he led the league in scoring. The Yankees also added an X-factor with the great University of Illinois runner Buddy Young. Coach Ray Flaherty started Young at fullback, which was rather unusual for a man who stood all of 5'5" and weighed 170 pounds.

But the Yanks' offensive system did not call for pass blocking or runs up the gut from this position. "His speed and deception made him the ideal man...and we complemented one another," said Sanders of Young.

Sanders rushed for 250 yards in a game against the hapless Rockets and passed for another touchdown, while Young returned a kickoff 95 yards. Unfortunately, Flaherty never came up with a passing attack to match his ground game, and the Browns cruised home again, 14-3.

But 1948 was the ultimate season for the Browns. More of the essential blocks had fallen into place. Frank Gatski was now the full-time center. Lou Saban had become an All-Pro at linebacker, as had Lou Rymkus at right tackle. (The two Lous would go on to coach against each other in the first year of the American Football League, with Rymkus winning the championship with Houston, and Saban later taking Buffalo to two league titles. Other future coaches on this Browns roster were Alex Agase and Ara Parseghian. All those playbook tests must have paid off.)

Tommy James, another of the old Massillon and Ohio State boys, was installed at cornerback, working opposite Warren Lahr, who would be a fixture in the Browns defensive backfield for years. One more former Massillon Tiger, Horace Gillom, was brought in to take care of the punting. With Lou Groza, Gillom would form one of the most formidable kicking combinations in football history.

Chubby Grigg came in at defensive tackle. At 275 pounds he was a giant for the times. Making games even nastier for opposing linemen was his habit of spitting tobacco juice in their faces before the snap.

But the biggest addition may have been Dub Jones, the element that made the Cleveland short passing game virtually unstoppable. Brown invented the position of flankerback for him. Jones could either be set outside the end in a running back position or placed in motion. He was tall for a halfback, which appealed to Brown. Combined with Dante Lavelli and Mac Speedie, Jones gave the team three big, fast receivers, the core idea of the future West Coast offense.

Jones had been a running back at Tulane University. The Cardinals made him their number-one draft pick in 1946, but he chose to join the ill-fated Miami Seahawks. When they folded, he moved on to the Brooklyn Dodgers, which was under the same ownership as the baseball team.

Branch Rickey handled the general manager's job for both franchises. With strong ties to the University of Michigan, he coveted the school's All-American tailback Bob Chappuis, whom the Browns had drafted. Brown managed to trade those rights for Jones and got $25,000 besides. He referred to it as the slickest deal he ever pulled off. Within a year, the football Dodgers were history, and Rickey was making his deals only with baseball players.

With this collection of stars, no one could match the Browns. The 49ers came close twice, losing by just seven and three points. Their game at Cleveland broke another attendance record, as 82,769 came to watch.

But that turned out to be a high-water mark. Neither the Browns nor the league would ever draw those kinds of numbers again. The championship game with Buffalo, which ended in a 49–7 rout, attracted only 23,000 fans to the big stadium.

It was the first time a professional team ever finished with a perfect record. The Bears had twice gone undefeated in the regular season, but then they lost the championship game.

Unfortunately for the Browns players, the winner's share from the championship was just $594.18, approximately 40 percent of what it had been two years prior.

The AAFC was clearly in trouble, and part of the problem was traceable to the fact that the Browns were just too good for their own good. With the Dodgers gone, the league shrank to seven teams in 1949. The teams were placed in one division with a 12-game schedule, and there would be a four-team playoff to determine a champion.

The fans weren't buying it. Only once did the Browns draw more than 31,000 to a home game, and that was because they were in the unusual position of having their supremacy threatened.

Their unbeaten string of 29 games came crashing down in San Francisco when they were mauled by the 49ers, 56–28. This was unquestionably the second best franchise in the league. In the first three years of the AAFC the 49ers had been in the same division as the Browns but could never get past them. The San Fransisco team played the Browns tough almost every time, though. Along with their West Coast partners, the Dons, the 49ers were the only AAFC team to beat Cleveland.

The 49ers had added Joe "the Jet" Perry to boost their running game as a complement to Frankie Albert's deadly passing. But no one had expected this rout of the Browns.

Brown was furious. "If you don't bounce back, there'll be some changes made, and that's cold turkey" he told the team. He spoke quietly, which made it all the more unnerving to this room full of stars.

"I'll get rid of anyone who can't block or tackle and replace him with a player who can."

The chastened Browns then destroyed the Dons in Los Angeles, 61–14, and knocked off San Francisco in the home rematch, 30–28.

The first round of the playoffs actually had a bit of a subplot because Buffalo had managed to tie Cleveland twice during the season. But the Bills were brushed aside, 31–21, with a paltry 17,000 at the stadium.

On December 11, the Browns finished off the 49ers, 21–7, and again the crowd barely filled one quarter of the big stadium. It was a fairly perfunctory affair. Motley ran 68 yards to break it open, and Jones sealed it with a fourth-quarter touchdown. The winner's share was a paltry $266.11.

It was the inglorious end of the AAFC, the final game in its history. A few weeks prior, the announcement was made that the league was folding. Three of its franchises, however, would move into the NFL: the 49ers, the Colts, and the Cleveland Browns.

The merger wasn't a complete victory for the 10-team older league. The NFL was far from secure. The AAFC had done significant financial damage to its franchises in Los Angeles and New York. The Pittsburgh Steelers, Green Bay Packers, and Detroit Lions were struggling. The

Boston Yanks had been folded into the New York Bulldogs, who were equally horrible.

NFL commissioner Bert Bell feared that fresh money from Texas might be coming into the AAFC, too. So peace talks began late in 1949.

Brown understood the irony of the situation. Just as in Massillon, he had built too well and run out of worlds to conquer. Without competition there can be no sports. He had genuine concern that he had placed his own financial future at risk by being too successful.

Brown took an active role in the negotiations, insisting that the AAFC teams enter the NFL as full and equal partners. They were awarded college draft picks for 1950 and were given the right to choose players from the folded AAFC franchises. But they were not permitted to keep any college players they had previously drafted as future selections. So the Browns were forced to give up the rights to Y.A. Tittle, Doak Walker, and Lynn Chandnois. Brown resented it, but that turned out to be the price of admission.

He did manage to salvage offensive guard Abe Gibron from Buffalo. And extracting end Len Ford from the wreckage of the Dons soon had enormous implications for the Browns' entire defensive scheme.

Most of the NFL owners welcomed the end of the battle. The exception was Washington Redskins owner George Preston Marshall. He once claimed that "the weakest team in the NFL can handle anyone in that league." He was furious that the AAFC had placed a team in Baltimore and that this interloper now was to be admitted to his league. He regarded the Colts as poachers on his territory and wanted to make it as rough as possible for the newcomers.

Marshall focused first on the Browns. Plans called for Cleveland to be placed in a division with Pittsburgh, Philadelphia, New York, the Chicago Cardinals...and Washington. Despite his expressed scorn for the AAFC, Marshall didn't care to compete directly with its four-time champions. There were to be 13 teams in the NFL in 1950, and he wanted Cleveland to play a round-robin schedule for the entire 12 games.

Brown wouldn't hear of it. He understood the pitfalls of playing an unfamiliar opponent for 12 straight weeks. To appease Marshall, however, the league made Baltimore go this route. The Colts finished 1–11 and promptly disappeared, only to resurface in 1953 as an entirely different franchise.

Marshall's apprehensions about the Browns were not widely shared in the NFL. The general take on the three new teams was that they would be exposed as strictly minor league, and very soon. In fact, just to bring that day nearer, Bell scheduled Cleveland's first game in the NFL against the league's two-time defending champions, the Philadelphia Eagles. It would be played on Philly's home field, too.

The NFL then settled back with a smirk and prepared to watch Brown get pasted. Bell, especially, relished the thought. He had been one of the founders of the Philadelphia franchise when it entered the league in 1933, and he had suffered through several seasons when it was the NFL doormat. But things began turning around after the team hired Greasy Neale as its head coach.

Neale had compiled a remarkable career. He played end at tiny West Virginia Wesleyan College and caught 14 passes in its upset of the University of West Virginia in 1912. He went on to play pro football with Jim Thorpe's Canton Bulldogs and pro baseball as an outfielder with the Cincinnati Reds. He started all eight games of the infamous 1919 World Series and led the team in hitting with a .357 average—although it should be pointed out that some of the Chicago White Sox pitchers weren't really trying.

Neale took obscure Washington and Jefferson College to the 1922 Rose Bowl as a coach and then became head coach at both West Virginia and the University of Virginia. By the time he arrived in Philadelphia in 1941, he was convinced that the T formation was the future of pro football. He made an exhaustive study of the game films from the Bears' 73–0 walloping of Washington in the previous year's championship game to figure out how Chicago made it work so well and how he could improve on it.

Within three years, he had it covered. The forlorn Eagles were up to second place in their division, and in three more seasons they were playing for the championship. They had won the last two NFL title games by shutouts, beating the Cardinals, 7–0, in a blizzard and the Rams, 14–0, in California sunshine. The Eagles were only the second team in modern NFL history to win back-to-back championships.

The Eagles were, in fact, the NFL counterpart to the Browns, with a 20–3–1 record over the previous two seasons. Neale had them playing old-school style, with an intimidating defensive line and a punishing running attack led by All-Pro Steve Van Buren.

A future Hall of Fame inductee, end Pete Pihos was the key to their minimalist passing game. Another of the game's immortals, Chuck Bednarik, had just come aboard as a linebacker. Bednarik would hang around long enough to start on the 1960 Eagles championship team and be acclaimed as the last of the league's 60-minute men, playing center on offense as well as linebacker.

Both the Eagles' defense, anchored by Bucko Kilroy and Mike Jarmoluk on the line, and their offense was ranked first in the league.

"This is the best team ever put together," said Neale. "All the Browns do is throw the ball."

The game was scheduled for a Sunday night, and for a few days it even took the big-league pennant races off the top of the sports pages—a rare event for September 1950. It was even more remarkable in Philadelphia because the "Whiz Kid" Phillies were going after the team's first pennant in 35 years.

Beyond dispute, baseball was the top professional sport in America. The NBA was just four years old and still learning to toddle. Hockey appealed to people in six cities, and two of them were in Canada. Football was a very distant second in fan interest. As one publication put it, this was the "bread and butter game," lacking the color and emotion of the college version.

Brown had hired the band director at Massillon, George Bird, to come up to Cleveland. Brown gave him the title of entertainment director and told him to put some kick in the halftime shows. Bird even hired a little person to dress up in a Brownie outfit as a team mascot, the sort of folderol in which pro teams of that day did not usually indulge. But Brown figured that the practice of giving football fans a full day's worth of entertainment for their money would work in Cleveland as well as it had in Massillon.

But the upcoming game in Philadelphia had a huge curiosity factor going for it. No one knew what to expect.

Van Buren was out of the lineup, resting a surgically repaired big toe. Still, would the Eagles really need to be 100 percent for the Browns? Not many thought so.

The run-up to the game might be compared to the first meeting between Russia's championship hockey team and the NHL All-Stars. Two different styles of play and life experience were going to collide. The result would be shocking.

"About 75,000 fans will pay more than $300,000 to watch a couple of championship teams that never met before," wrote *The Plain Dealer*'s beat reporter, Harold Sauerbrei, "because the NFL steadfastly refused to recognize the AAFC."

It still didn't really give the AAFC's teams their due. In some NFL press guides, players from the AAFC were listed as having "no previous professional experience."

The expert opinion was that the Cleveland defense was not strong enough to stop the Eagles' running attack. But the Philadelphia defense, which had stymied every passer in the NFL, would stop Otto Graham, too. It had thrown quarterbacks for 359 yards in losses the previous years. Most of them were coverage sacks. In Neale's scheme, both a linebacker and a defensive back were positioned across from the opponents' top pass receivers and wouldn't let them off the line of scrimmage.

Even Cleveland partisans didn't think the Browns would be able to pass. In the college All-Star game, though, Charlie "Choo Choo" Justice had been able to get outside the Eagles defense on pitchouts. Sauerbrei felt Brown had something like that planned, too.

All these suppositions were wrong. The Eagles were simply overmatched in every aspect of the 35–10 game.

At one point, Brown got on the phone with assistant coach Blanton Collier in the press box. "How are they covering our receivers?" Brown asked.

"Truthfully, I don't know," Collier responded. "I can't tell because I'm sure they don't know what they're trying to do themselves."

"Jeez, they've got a lotta guns, haven't they?" said an almost dazed Neale afterward. "A lotta guns."

Pihos walked out of the silent Philadelphia locker room and told reporters, "We just met up with a team from the big league."

The Eagles' defensive plan had worked as long as it was confronted by one or two big receivers. But the Browns had three or four, and Philadelphia didn't know where the next strike was coming from. They had never seen anything like this. When Lavelli and Speedie were chucked at the line, Graham simply found Jones and halfback Rex Bumgardner running free. Graham completed 21 passes for 346 yards.

Philadelphia's top defender, Russ Craft, was covering Jones, who caught a quick succession of short-out patterns. When Craft began cheating up on the coverage, Jones simply broke downfield, and Graham hit him with a 59-yard bomb. Then Graham found Lavelli and Speedie breaking away from the confused Philadelphia defense.

Brown had noticed something important in the game films. Rather than going wide, he saw that the Eagles were most vulnerable up the gut.

Neale depended on his big defensive line to stop the running game because he was putting two linebackers wide on receivers. Brown saw that the Eagles linemen were taking their splits according to the way the offensive line set up.

So as the game progressed, Brown instructed his offensive line to move imperceptibly farther apart on each play. Just by a half step or so.

Within a few snaps, the Eagles line had been spread wide enough for Motley to come thundering through its middle. When Philadelphia tried to correct that, the Browns sent Jones running wide on a 57-yard run. The dazed Eagles defenders then tried to cover the big Cleveland ends one on one. Graham sliced that up easily.

Brown had heard Neale's sneering remark and said, "I wanted to show him we could do more than pass. But we are not going to gloat over this. There is a long season ahead."

"That is the best football team I have ever seen," said Bell.

"Graham is the ideal player," added Neale. "He hangs the ball up there and lets his receivers go get it. We couldn't control them."

When it was suggested to him that his team couldn't overcome the loss of Van Buren, he shook his head. "Maybe it would have been a touchdown or two closer," he said. "But we wouldn't have won."

Speedie was given the game ball, as he had been in the first game of every season. It was a custom that went back to 1946, when he scored the first touchdown in Browns history.

Columnist Gordon Cobbledick wrote that the Browns "had experienced few games in the AAFC in which they were so completely the masters." That was a small exaggeration. But it was understandable payback, too.

"The team that was considered inferior by a good many cocky partisans of the NFL," editorialized *The Plain Dealer*, "whipped the pants off that league's best."

In many respects, the only comparable game in football history was the New York Jets beating the Baltimore Colts in Super Bowl III, more than 18 years later.

That game, too, gave immediate credibility to a maligned league. But in that case, the American Football League was still alive to be totally wrapped into the NFL. In 1950 the AAFC could only receive posthumous respect.

But the Browns had entered in the NFL and knocked the door down upon their arrival. It would not be shut again for years to come.

10

1950: Cleveland Browns 30, Los Angeles Rams 28

Paul Brown was right about foregoing the gloating until later. Cleveland would not go unscathed in its first season.

Their former AAFC partners, the Baltimore Colts, gave them no problem in the second game. But in the first home game as part of the new league, the New York Giants came into the Lakefront and shut them out, 6–0.

It was the first shutout, the first time they had failed to score a touchdown, in the team's history. Otto Graham and Marion Motley collided on a botched handoff near the Giants' goal, and New York recovered the fumble. That was the Browns' only real threat.

Still, over the course of a season these things can happen. It did give reinforcement, however, to those who figured that the Philly game was a fluke and hoped the Browns would collapse.

Brown was not fooled. Despite all the praise showered on his team after its humiliation of the Eagles, he knew the animosity still ran deep.

Three weeks later, it happened again. This time the Giants won by a 17–13 score. Brown came in for second-guessing by kicking a field goal on first down from the 10-yard line with 25 seconds to play in the first half. But an even bigger factor was that the Giants intercepted Graham six times. Not once was he able to sustain a drive, the only Cleveland touchdown coming after a fumble recovered at the New York goal line.

Both teams finished the season at 10-2. So in their first year in the NFL, the Browns were involved in a divisional playoff.

Coach Steve Owen had put together a formidable defense in New York. Five of his starters would go on to the Pro Bowl, and another, Tom Landry, became one of the great defensive minds in NFL history with the Dallas Cowboys.

The Giants never gave up more than 21 points all year. Then midway through the season Owen had a brainstorm that transformed his offense. He began to use two completely different backfields, one with Charlie Conerly as tailback in what was called the A formation, and the other with Travis Tidwell at quarterback in the T formation. The Giants alternated their running backs, too. Suddenly a fairly mediocre offense was unstoppable. They had lost two early games when they couldn't score a touchdown. But once Owen unveiled the new plan, the Giants racked up 157 points in just three games.

Even though the Giants had beaten them twice and were now a far more formidable team on offense, the home-field advantage gave Cleveland a slight edge among the oddsmakers. For this was surely going to be a defensive struggle.

The winter of 1950 was starting off as one of the most brutal in Ohio's history. Michigan and Ohio State had played in a November blizzard in Columbus, the Wolverines winning, 9-3, without ever making a first down. The same weather pattern prevailed into December. The Browns had their rematch against Philadelphia on December 3. The game was played in a freezing rain. Cleveland won 13-7 and did not throw a single pass.

It was the last time that ever was done in the NFL. Some observers felt Brown was still out to prove a point against Neale and his other detractors in the league, although Brown never admitted it.

Despite the jeers that Cleveland was playing basketball on grass, Brown's team really lived off the speed of its defense. The Browns defense was built upon two players: Bill Willis in the middle and Len Ford as a pass-rushing end.

Almost every pro team used a five-man defensive line at this time, with three linebackers and three backs. But Willis was so fast that

Brown felt he could drop him off the line and play a 4-3-4 alignment. In essence, the position of middle guard was invented for Willis. His assignment was either to strike at the point of attack or drop back into pass coverage. He became the most disruptive force in the Browns defense, and when the opposition began double-teaming him, it left Ford free to wreak his havoc.

Ford was 30 pounds heavier than Willis and almost as quick. In the AAFC, the Dons had used him on offense, too, and he caught 67 passes in his two years with them. The Browns were pretty well set at that position. But his defensive skills, the speed with which he could get to opposing quarterbacks, is what enabled the 4-3-4 defense to work. Opponents had to keep a back at home to block him, and that simplified downfield coverage for the Browns.

"Really blows in," read a Detroit Lions scouting report on him. "Does a lot of jumping over blockers.... Plays inside very tough. Must be blocked, or he will kill the passer. He claims there is no one in the league who can take him out alone."

All of this came boiling over in the first game with the Cardinals. Just two seasons away from playing in the title game, they were on a downward slope by 1950, and Ford was giving them an especially hard time. Fullback Pat Harder was assigned to slow him up once he came off the line. Harder couldn't handle it. Ford broke through him to the quarterback time after time. What happened then remains one of the most bitterly debated incidents in NFL history.

According to the Browns, the frustrated Harder waited until Ford had passed him and then deliberately smashed him in the side of his face with an elbow. There were no face masks in those days, no protection against the blow. It crushed Ford's cheekbone, broke his nose, and took out several of his teeth. He underwent extensive surgery, and for a time it wasn't known if he would ever play again.

What further infuriated the Browns was that Harder was not penalized on the play. Instead, incredibly, the officials penalized the prostrate Ford for illegal use of hands and said that he had precipitated the incident.

Brown took the game films to the commissioner's office. Bert Bell agreed that Ford had not been to blame. He added, however, that he would not penalize or suspend Harder. Instead, he put out an order that things like this really had to stop.

Brown was sure that the mild treatment of the case was further proof of the resentment the NFL harbored toward his team. Bell had told the coach after the game in Philadelphia that he was "genuinely pleased" the Browns had played so well because they made the entire league stronger and more competitive. But his reaction to Ford's injury proved otherwise, Brown thought.

Brown would use the discrimination to stiffen the resolve of the Browns and foster the us-against-the-world outlook that can motivate a team. But he still didn't have Ford in the lineup.

Ford shrugged off the violent foul later in the year.

"You just have to expect some of the rough stuff every game," he said. "I just didn't duck, that's all."

But the injury also planted an idea in Brown's fertile mind. What if Ford had been wearing a protective mask over his face?

Protective equipment came slowly to football. Helmets date back to the 1890s. Prior to that, players protected their heads by growing their hair long. Leather headgear was not required in college football until 1939, and not in the NFL until 1943. Some macho members of the 1940 champion Bears team were still playing bare-headed.

Future president Gerald Ford played center for Michigan without a helmet in the early 1930s. It was a fact that Lyndon B. Johnson would eagerly seize upon years later to make a widely printed wisecrack about Ford's mental capacity.

The technology for an improved plastic helmet existed by 1940. But when the war came, plastic was reserved for military use. Not until the last years of the decade was the right material available for helmet production. The use of plastic allowed for the addition of a face guard because the plastic had the strength to support the bolt needed to hold the mask to the helmet. But only players who were injured wore them. To seek such protection otherwise was the mark of a wuss.

Another helmet addition made possible by plastic was the use of a team insignia baked onto the side. The first franchise to sport such a look was the Los Angeles Rams. Their stylized horns were first displayed in 1948 and have remained a part of the team's visual identity ever since, even after its move to St. Louis.

After Ford's injury, Brown knew the only way he'd get him back in the 1950 season was by devising a mask. Makeshift masks were not unknown, but they were unstable. There had to be a better way of protecting the players. It was something to ponder.

The field at Lakefront Stadium was frozen solid when the Giants came in for the December 17 playoff. Another snowstorm had hit two days prior, and roads south of the city were almost impassable.

The climate in Columbus had also turned chilly: Wes Fesler was on his way out as Ohio State's coach. Even though he had lost to the University of Michigan in the most abominable weather conditions in the history of the series, a loss to Michigan was still a loss to Michigan. Rumors were swirling that Brown was headed back as athletic director and head coach. Newspapers were even reporting that a powerful group of alumni had formed to block the move because he had turned his back on the university before.

If the offer had come one year before, with the AAFC foundering and Brown worried about his future, he may have considered it. But by now the time for returning to Columbus had passed forever. The Buckeyes, instead, hired Woody Hayes from Miami University, with historic results.

But amidst the chill of Fesler's losing in Columbus and the frozen gridiron at the Lakefront, the Browns still had to face the Giants for the playoff, and the Browns ended up in a fight for their lives. Lou Groza kicked an early field goal, and then the Browns hung on. They had to stop New York six times on plays inside their 10 yard line.

Sportswriters described the atmosphere as resembling a college game, with the crowd chanting "Hold that line" each time the Giants threatened. That was just the sort of atmosphere Brown wanted to foster in the professional game. But he was far too busy to notice.

Once again the Giants had been able to thwart the Browns' passing attack, limiting it to just 43 yards on three completions. They made just nine first downs.

Then in the fourth quarter, with the ball on the Cleveland 36, New York sent halfback Gene Roberts on a simple run up the middle. Bouncing off his blockers, he suddenly found an open seam and was streaking downfield with no one in front of him. Willis, however, was behind him and closing the gap fast. The lineman ran the halfback down at the Cleveland 4, the Browns held again, and the Giants had to kick a tying field goal rather than going ahead.

Those who saw it say it was the greatest defensive play they ever had witnessed. "Where There's a Willis There's a Way," read the headline in one Cleveland paper. After the game, Brown called Willis "the greatest lineman in American football." It remains one of the most celebrated plays in Browns history, a season-saving effort by the man who ended up being voted the team's Most Valuable Player.

With the winter wind in New York's face, the following kickoff was short. Then Graham took over the game.

So much attention has been paid to his skill as a passer that it is generally forgotten that Graham was also an excellent runner, one of the fastest men of the era at his position. The concept of a drop-back passer who can also use his speed as a weapon—the Donovan McNabb–Michael Vick model—is supposed to be a development of the contemporary game. But Graham was fast enough to play defensive back. And when the occasion demanded it, he could change the course of a game by running the ball.

This was one of those times. As the Giants bunched up to stop Motley from coming up the middle, Brown used the big fullback as a decoy and ran Graham wide. In three plays Graham picked up 36 yards, and the Browns were sitting on the New York 29 with 58 seconds to play.

Enter, "the Toe." With the wind gusting from behind, Groza sent his second field goal of the game through the uprights. The Giants protested, claiming the kick had sailed wide. But the officials ruled it had been blown to the side only after going through the goalposts.

A few seconds later, Willis and the entire Cleveland front burst through on Conerly and tackled him in the end zone for the safety. Final score: 8–3.

In three games, the Giants had given up one touchdown to the best offense in the NFL. But they were going home, and the Cleveland defense was taking the Browns to the title game.

The front page of Monday's papers featured a three-column shot of Groza, with his bare right foot extended smack into the lens of the camera.

A legend was being born. In one more week, the most celebrated toe in football would become magnified even more.

The Rams were returning to Cleveland for the first time, and everything was on the line.

Brown had always looked for speed in his players. But in the Rams he would be facing a track team. They were regarded as the fastest team in the history of football, with eight players who could break 10 seconds for the 100-yard dash. Among those eight were Tom Fears, who had shattered the NFL record for receptions in a season, and Elroy "Crazylegs" Hirsch, at the other end, who was even more dangerous as a runner after he caught the ball. Glenn Davis, the famed "Mr. Outside" of the national champion Army teams of the 1940s, was back from his military service and running out of the Rams' halfback slot. Bob Boyd and Verda "Vitamin T." Smith would go out as flankers, and both had been track stars in college.

The Rams were so deep they put both of their quarterbacks on the All-Pro team. Bob Waterfield was the starter when the team had been in Cleveland and passed the Rams to the 1945 title. Many sportswriters, however, were more impressed by the fact that he would be joined at the championship game by his wife, Jane Russell.

Waterfield was sharing duties with young Norm Van Brocklin, who had learned the T formation at the University of Oregon under an old friend of Brown's from high school days. Jimmy Aiken had moved on from Canton McKinley High School and turned the Ducks into a top team in the Pacific Coast Conference, with an invitation to the 1949 Cotton Bowl.

The Rams' combination had passed for 29 touchdowns, while sharing time almost equally. Van Brocklin had the slight statistical edge, but Coach Joe Stydahar felt Waterfield's experience could hold the advantage in the title game. He got the start.

The Rams had another thing going for them, too. The NFL rules on tackling were far more liberal in 1950. Even when a ball carrier went down by contact, if the tackle was not made secure, he could get right up and start running again. The rule worked to the advantage of the Rams. They might be knocked off balance by an arm tackle, but with their tremendous speed, they popped up and were off to the races.

The Rams simply overwhelmed their opposition that season, scoring 466 points, an average of 39 per game. They had run up 70 on the Colts, 65 on the Lions, 51 on the Packers.

On the other hand, their defense could stop hardly anyone. The Bears beat them twice and forced a playoff, which the Rams had won 24–14. The Eagles hit them with 56 points in the Rams' other loss of the year. They ranked ninth of the 13 teams in defensive statistics, giving up at least two touchdowns in every game. By contrast, the Browns had given up more than 14 points just four times all season.

Strangely enough, Stydahar was regarded as a defensive specialist. But there is a maxim in football that teams relying on the pass as their principal weapon seldom play good defense. The Rams were proof of that. Seventy-seven percent of the yardage they had gained this year came by the pass. They favored the bomb. While the basis of the Browns passing attack relied on Graham's precision on short patterns, Waterfield and Van Brocklin just let 'er rip.

Over and above the contrast in styles was the drama of the fugitive Rams returning to the city they had abandoned. A cartoon in *The Plain Dealer* depicted Waterfield astride a charging ram, with Fears and Van Brocklin seated beside him. "Back to my old stomping ground," read the caption over Waterfield's head. In the corner of the drawing was Brown saying, "We've waited five years for this."

That was the attitude in Cleveland. Forget the fact that Dan Reeves had taken the Rams west only because he knew that his team couldn't compete with the Paul Brown mystique. This game was going to be about payback.

For all of that, however, Lakefront Stadium was less than half full. The Rams had drawn 83,500 supporters to the Los Angeles Coliseum for their playoff game against the Bears the previous weekend, while the Browns had only 33,000 for their game with New York. True, it had been sunny and 92 degrees in California, while Cleveland fans had to sit through a wind chill in the single digits. But crowds of 80,000 and more used to watch the Browns play in the early years of the AAFC. They weren't coming close to that figure anymore.

Columnist Gordon Cobbledick didn't have a problem with that. He felt the Browns had developed a "solid core" of fans, as distinguished from the "sensation-hunters and curiosity-seekers who contributed to notable stadium crowds."

He couldn't very well call those fans front-runners because the Browns were always running in front. But a pro football game was no longer regarded as the place to be seen in Cleveland. It did not have that certain cachet.

Browns owner Arthur McBride spoke hopefully of a time when maybe 50,000 fans would come to the home games. But that seemed like wishful thinking. For one thing, television was still in its infancy in giving the sport exposure. The Browns had put some of their games on the DuMont Network affiliate as early as 1948. Each team was expected to make a television deal for itself, and the money was not so hot. The contract to televise the Browns-Rams game on a national hookup brought in just $45,000, according to commissioner Bell. It would be blacked out in a 75-mile radius of Cleveland. Bell said the league had been offered a paltry $1,500 for local rights, and he had turned it down as unworthy. He felt the hit the game would take at the gate if it were shown for free was worth more than that.

In contrast, today, each of the 32 teams in the NFL will make $115 million each year under the terms of the league's television contract signed in 2005. Back in 1950, this sort of money was unimaginable. Television was definitely growing fast, but a 16-inch set was priced at nearly $400, the equivalent of $2,500 today after inflation.

In addition, the coaxial cable that would link the West Coast to the rest of the country in a truly national TV network wasn't completed until 1951. Fans in Los Angeles and Cleveland could not watch their teams compete in this game.

The rules were still being drawn up. A station in Erie, Pennsylvania, had sued the league because it was not permitted to carry the game. This struck Cobbledick as patently absurd.

"The privilege of watching a game on television from the comfort of one's easy chair seems to have become a right," he wrote. "But unrestricted televising of Browns games might mean the financial ruin of the Steelers and the Lions. It would mean the end of organized commercial sports."

Seldom has a writer been more wrong. Television would lead to the greatest expansion in sports history and riches beyond comprehension for the NFL. But in 1950 no one could have predicted that.

More snow had fallen during the week, and it was expected that the field again would be frozen. These conditions seemed to favor the Browns, and they were made three point favorites.

It was also announced that Ford would play with a mask protecting his face. That would give Cleveland a boost on its pass rush. If the Browns couldn't put pressure on Waterfield, there would be deep trouble.

As it turned out, the weather took a turn for the good. On the morning after Christmas the temperature was 29 degrees, although a wind gusting at 28 miles per hour made it seem a lot colder than that. The final attendance count was just 29,751.

This is one of those games that if everyone who claimed to have been in the stadium actually was there, it would have sold out by a factor of three.

It was a classic in every sense of the word, and at its end, Browns fans rushed the field and tore the goalposts down. It stirred that kind of passion.

Even the imperturbable Brown was visibly shaken after the 30–28 result was in.

It had been a roller-coaster ride, and just when Cleveland's final hope appeared to have been extinguished, Graham found a way to win. The quarterback would win seven championships in his 10 years in Cleveland. But to many Browns fans, this was his finest hour.

On the first Rams play from scrimmage, Waterfield hit Davis on an 82-yard scoring strike. It happened so fast that Cleveland fans couldn't quite believe it. Maybe the Los Angeles attack really was unstoppable. Graham came right back, though, and on his first possession he found Dub Jones for a touchdown. Then Waterfield hit Lavelli for 37 yards.

Back and forth it went, but bad things continued to happen to the Browns. The automatic Groza missed a point after, and instead of being tied at the half, the Browns trailed, 14–13.

The tireless Mac Speedie was playing with a pulled leg muscle and never returned in the second half. The reliable Motley fumbled, and the Rams scooped it up and returned it 6 yards for their fourth touchdown.

But Waterfield was picked off five times by the Browns. In one sequence of plays, Ford crashed through and threw three different Rams back for 38 yards in losses. Even with that, Waterfield ran up 312 yards in passing, and as the fourth quarter began, Los Angeles led 28–20.

Then Graham began finding Dante Lavelli on a series of short passes. As the Rams defense overcompensated, Rex Bumgardner eluded all coverage in the back of the end zone. The score was 28–27 with 10 minutes left.

Cleveland got the ball back, and once more Graham began moving the team down the field. As they crossed the 30, he called a quarterback draw. Brown knew that the Rams were stacked to stop Motley, and this play was a variation on Cleveland's basic draw. Brown claimed it originated by accident when Graham couldn't make a clean handoff to Motley in a game earlier in the season and kept the ball himself. However it happened, it was effective, and that's what Brown called for now.

But as Graham reached the 25 he was hit from the blind side and fumbled, the third time Cleveland coughed up the ball. The Rams took over. There were three minutes to go.

"I wanted to die right there," the quarterback said afterward. "We were throwing the game away. Of course, we had to get ours the hard way."

Brown realized the time for coaching was past. It was now a time when an inner fire takes over, when his team either had it or it didn't. He walked over to the disconsolate Graham and firmly promised that the Cleveland defense would get the ball back for him.

He was right. The Rams were forced to punt. Cliff Lewis gathered it in on his own 19 and brought it out to the 32. Seventy seconds to play.

Graham only needed 50 of them.

He rolled out for a 14-yard run. He hit Bumgardner for 15 yards. The ball now was in Rams territory, on the 39.

Graham passed to Jones for 16 yards. Then he passed to Bumgardner again for 12—short throws, hitting the Rams from every conceivable direction.

The ball was on the 11. Graham carried the ball once more to position it in the middle of the field. Twenty seconds to play, and Groza trotted onto the field. He had broken a tie the previous week with 58 seconds to go. But this time the kick was to win or lose the championship.

"I was just going over the fundamentals," he said in the clubhouse. Then he looked over at Joe Page, the veteran relief pitcher for the Yankees, who had come into the room to join in the celebration. "Ask him. You don't get nervous in a tight spot like that."

Page shook his head in disbelief. "Like hell," he said. "Don't tell me you weren't worried about missing. I know what was going through your mind."

Groza's fundamentals were sound, and the Browns were champions again.

"Justice and Joy Came to the Boys from the Wrong Side of the Tracks," read the lead on the game story.

The editorial page recalled former NFL comissioner Elmer Layden's remark of five years before when he laughed off the AAFL: "First let them buy a football." Well, according to the paper, "The boys didn't have to go buy a football. They already had one, and they knew quite a bit about using it.... The flag of the late lamented AAFC flies high, and Paul Brown has the last laugh."

"This is the gamest bunch of guys in the world," said Brown, his gray felt hat battered out of recognition but still on his head. "Next to my wife and family, these guys are my life. I never gave up hope. I know this gang too well. I know they never quit. This is the greatest football team a coach ever had, and there was never a game like this one."

Brown may have been right. In just eight more years, however, the Colts and Giants would play their overtime title game, which was immediately labeled as the greatest game in history. It had been televised nationally, after all. Millions watched it.

The classic championship game of 1950 was seen by a comparative handful. It slowly faded from the national memory, part of the hazy past, the visual images losing focus. But it remains a shining memory in Cleveland and wherever Browns fans gather.

With this victory, Brown had coached a championship team at every level of football competition. No coach up to that time had won both a collegiate and professional title. (And none would again until

Jimmy Johnson, and then Barry Switzer, accomplished the feat with the Dallas Cowboys in the early 1990s.)

In his previous 16 seasons, Brown had coached 12 champions. This one may have been the sweetest of them all.

11

1954: Cleveland Browns 56, Detroit Lions 10

"Why would he want to leave?" asked Browns owner Arthur "Mickey" McBride after the 1950 title game. The rumors about Paul Brown returning to coach at Ohio State University were still lingering, and McBride wanted to put them to rest once and for all. "Paul Brown is the boss and answers to no one. He has the best football job in the country."

More than that, Brown's team still was defined by the core of players he had personally chosen back in 1946, the Ohio gang and their assorted friends: Otto Graham, Dante Lavelli, Marion Motley, Bill Willis, Lou Groza, Frank Gatski, Mac Speedie, Lou Rymkus, Lin Houston, Cliff Lewis, and defensive end George Young. These 11 had been with him all the way in Cleveland. As a result, the Browns retained the sort of collegiate spirit that their coach found most congenial. His methods worked best when he had that kind of player.

Six of them ended up in the Hall of Fame, along with Brown himself and Ford, who joined the team when it reached the NFL. Of the 16 members of the Browns organization currently in the Hall, eight were associated with this team. To the end of his life, Brown insisted that Speedie's absence from the Hall was a grave injustice.

Speedie's story arc was as dramatic as any of the Browns', and a bit reminiscent of *Forrest Gump*. Speedie was diagnosed with Perthes disease as a child. This is a degenerative disease of the hip socket and can lead to permanent disability, with one leg being shorter than the other. When Speedie was diagnosed, the only known treatment was leg braces and rest. His parents were told that he probably would have to wear the braces for the rest of his life.

He said in later life that his desire to excel was fed by his illness. In a 1982 interview he said, "I spent so much time eating my heart out because I couldn't play normally that when they took the brace off (after four years)...it was like turning a frisky colt out to pasture after a year in a box stall. I had such a backlog of athletic ambition that I wanted to play football, basketball, and track all at one time."

Speedie did all three at the University of Utah and always claimed his experience in running hurdles was critical in developing the balance and timing he needed as a receiver. His career stats compare favorably to those of Tom Fears, Elroy Hirsch, and Pete Pihos—three receivers who are in the Hall. But Speedie played just three seasons in the NFL, signing with the Canadian League in 1953, and that worked against him.

After five successive championships, the 11-man nucleus of Brown's team was starting to slow down. But Brown always said that cutting a player who had contributed a lot to his team was the worst part of his job.

In a few years, this core of veteran Browns was reduced by two more, and writers in other cities began referring to them disparagingly as the "nine old men." The phrase hearkened back to Franklin D. Roosevelt's description of the conservative U.S. Supreme Court in the late 1930s. But it appeared to be just as true in Cleveland.

Still, the Browns swept through an 11–1 season in 1951, winning every game after a loss in San Francisco in the opener. The dynasty seemed as secure as ever.

But an odd thing happened in Los Angeles that December. They lost to the Rams for the championship, 24–17, the first time the Browns had ever been on the wrong end of the score in the final game of the season.

The Browns had knocked off Los Angeles by 15 points in an early season meeting at the Coliseum. The Rams also had been in a tight battle with the suddenly formidable Detroit Lions for the division title right up to the final weekend of the season. Cleveland thought the Rams would offer only minimal hindrance in their pursuit of six straight championship wins.

But the Rams had rebuilt their defense and were able to put pressure on Graham. One sack resulted in a fumble and a Rams touchdown, which was usually the Cleveland way of doing things. Graham came right back with a touchdown strike and after the Rams took a 17–10 lead in the fourth quarter, Ken Carpenter's 3-yard touchdown tied it for the Browns.

The Los Angeles coaching staff, however, had discovered a flaw in the Cleveland pass defense. It keyed on the opponent's fullback, and once the Browns safety saw to which side the fullback was going, he shifted in that direction. The Rams waited for the right time to take advantage. It came with the ball on Cleveland's 27 late in the fourth quarter. The Browns defense shifted with the Los Angeles flow, but wide receiver Fears cut back across the grain and caught a touchdown pass from Norm Van Brocklin before the Browns could recover.

Brown went to Harold Sauerbrei, *The Plain Dealer*'s beat writer, on the following day and strongly suggested he file a story placing the entire blame on the coach. He would not let his old pros, Lewis and Tommy James, take the fall. It was an unusual request, but beat writers knew the importance of staying on good terms with the old man.

Still, it had been a sour end to a fine season, and it rankled. Brown knew his team was getting older. Graham took a beating on most Sundays, and he wasn't going to last forever. But although Brown was deeply annoyed at the references to the "nine old men," he couldn't deny the basic truth.

There was also the problem of the balance sheet. In Browns lore, these great championship years were marked with consistent sellouts at the Lakefront. That just isn't true. Between 1950 and 1955, when the Browns won the divisional title every year, there was exactly one sellout at home. Most seasons they averaged approximately 40,000 spectators per game, less than half of the stadium's capacity. The top ticket price during most of this period was $3.60.

Sellouts were far less frequent throughout the league in these years. But the Rams, playing in a comparably sized stadium, often filled theirs. Cleveland's most intense rivals, the Giants, usually drew more when the Browns played in New York than they did when the game was in Cleveland. The Detroit Lions, playing in Briggs Stadium, with 25,000 fewer seats, sold out almost every game and consistently outdrew the Browns during this era.

A big part of the problem was Lakefront Stadium. It is usually described as *cavernous*, and that's as good a word as any. *Monstrosity* is also excellent.

Cleveland Stadium was built as part of the city's bid to get the 1932 Olympics—the same reason Los Angeles built its Coliseum. Los Angeles got the Games, though, and Cleveland got a white elephant.

The Indians tried playing there but after one season went back to old League Park. They returned downtown only on weekends, when crowds would be larger. When Bill Veeck took over management of the Indians he moved to Lakefront Stadium full time, and with a series of imaginative, and sometimes bizarre, promotions, he managed to fill it surprisingly often.

But the dimensions were gargantuan. Artificial fences helped make home runs possible, but fans seated in the outfield or deep in the upper deck may as well have been on the far side of Lake Erie. Moreover, a crowd of 35,000, a full house in many ballparks of that era, would get lost in this one.

As bad as Cleveland Stadium was for baseball, it was equally terrible for football. Several collegiate stadiums have greater seating capacities. For the most part, though, they are configured as bowls or horseshoes, with seats rising from the field at a steeper pitch but a nearer proximity. Intimacy was not part of the game plan in Cleveland.

To be fair, the big stadium in Los Angeles was not much better. Songwriter Johnny Mercer once noted in a bit of doggerel:

I went to a game at the Coliseum
My seats were so high I couldn't see 'em.
I asked my neighbor, "Are these seats legal?"
He said, "Don't ask me. I'm a bald eagle."

But the Coliseum was warmer. We like to believe that previous generations were made of sterner stuff than today's spectators. But sitting in a north wind howling in from the lake is not much fun. And 50 years ago, pro football simply did not have the kind of drawing power for its fans to tolerate those conditions, even in the most successful cities. However, today's fans in Green Bay, Chicago, and Cleveland now pack these places on frigid December days, while 50 years ago cold weather was given as the excuse for why championship games never came close to selling out in Cleveland.

Browns owner McBride had hoped for a greater showing for his team, regardless of the stadium. He wanted a core of 50,000 fans at a minimum, and the actual figures were a disappointment.

"I'm not in this business to make money," he said in a 1947 interview. "Cleveland has been good to me. I've made a great deal of money here. If I was looking for a get-rich-quick investment, the last thing I'd do is buy a pro football club. It's a risky business. Too much depends on ideal weather conditions, and this is no climate to risk a buck on a raindrop. I don't intend to lose a bundle, either. I just want to give the people of Cleveland the best team possible."

McBride sincerely believed that he was doing his civic duty by owning the Browns. Still, money was tight. Most players had to hold off-season jobs to get by, and Speedie could not pass up the contract offer in Canada.

McBride was an ideal owner as far as Brown was concerned, never interfering, giving the coach free rein. But this arrangement was nearing an end. Within two years, McBride decided that he'd had all of pro football he wanted.

While the newspapers had been filled with stories a few years prior about the buildup to the 1950 championship with the Rams, a small note in the Cleveland papers said that the Detroit Lions had hired a new coach. His name was Buddy Parker, and in a few years, Browns fans would learn to detest him. For the first time since Brown's frustrations against Canton McKinley High School almost 20 years prior, he had acquired a nemesis.

The Lions entered the NFL in 1934, after moving from Portsmouth, won a championship in their second season in Detroit, and hadn't been heard from since. Bo McMillin, a great college coach, was the latest in a succession of men who couldn't get the team turned around. Now it was Parker's shot.

He had been the backfield coach and was a link to the 1935 championship team, on which he had been a halfback. Parker had shown some ability when he was shoved into the head coach's job with the Chicago Cardinals midway through the 1949 season. He went 4-1-1 the rest of the way. But the Cards had a chance to hire the legendary Curly Lambeau from the Green Bay Packers, and Parker was sent packing.

He landed with the Lions, where things were starting to come together. McMillin had done a masterful job of assembling the core. With two high picks in the 1950 draft he had taken the previous two Heisman Trophy winners, Doak Walker of Southern Methodist University and Leon Hart of Notre Dame University. In the same draft was offensive guard Lou Creekmur of the College of William and Mary, who would go on to a Hall of Fame career. Running back Bob Hoernschemeyer, who had played for McMillin at Indiana University, was selected as a pick from the defunct AAFC.

But McMillin's master stroke was a trade for a new quarterback. Bobby Layne had been a tailback at the University of Texas. He was drafted by Pittsburgh, traded to the Bears, who were already set with passers, and then sent off to the woeful New York Bulldogs. This was a team so atrocious that Layne said the experience made him think of giving up football. McMillin, however, saw promise in him and sent off a local favorite, Bob Mann (who was also the Lions' first black player), to get Layne.

Parker, who also came from Texas, had a special affinity for Layne.
"He was a case of don't do as I do, but do as I tell you," said Parker.
"He was a one-man team who went against all the rules. But, by golly,
it worked."

With Layne setting the tone, the Lions became known throughout
the league as the best ongoing party in football. If anyone had tried to
set a curfew or a drinking ban on this team he would have faced a rev-
olution, if not a firing squad. Layne believed that the team that drank
together won together, and when he had a drink everyone had a drink.

There were reports that the smell of alcohol sometimes pervaded
the Lions huddle as he called the plays. Teammate Jimmy David denied
that ever happened "at least, not during the regular season." It should
be pointed out, however, that David played on the defensive unit.

"I wanted to start this book," Layne wrote in his ghosted autobiography, *Always on Sundays*, "by saying I was driving down the avenue
early one morning, alert and happy, when a parked car ran into me
head-on. But who would believe it?" When he was picked up, obviously
intoxicated, by a Detroit cop, he got off by arguing that the policeman
had mistaken his Texas drawl for slurred speech.

He was the temperamental opposite of the Browns' Graham,
whose nickname had become "Automatic Otto." Graham was consistent, calm, understood Brown's plan, and threw to a given spot better
than anyone in the game. Layne's passes wobbled, and there were times
when it seemed the Lions were playing one game and Layne was
involved in another. But in the fourth quarter, he was the most dangerous man in football. Expectations were enormous when the 1950
season began, and when the team ended up no better than 6–6,
McMillin was fired. The University of Michigan's Fritz Crisler was the
favorite to replace McMillin in the rumor factories, and the team's
board of directors would have liked that. The Lions were deep in the
red, and a local hero like Crisler would have given the team the same
sort of boost Cleveland received by hiring Brown. It didn't work out,
though, and the job instead went to Parker at about half of McMillin's
$30,000 annual salary.

In the next few years, Parker added more key elements, including defensive back Jack Christiansen from Colorado A&M (now Colorado State University) and Yale Lary from Texas A&M. Parker also brought in veterans Pat Harder and Vince Bannonis, whom he had coached with the Cardinals.

Mammoth Les Bingaman, billed as the biggest man in football at 315 pounds, was made into a middle guard as the Lions revamped their defense. Where Cleveland's Willis had reinvented the position because of his speed, Bingaman redefined it because of his sheer bulk. He was unblockable. No one came up the middle on Detroit.

The Lions just missed in 1951, losing twice late in the season to finish behind Los Angeles. But in 1952 they were ready.

The Lions whipped Los Angeles, 31–21, in a playoff, and the stage was set for the first championship meeting between the teams that would come to dominate the NFL of the early 1950s.

The two cities had a traditional rivalry in sports and many other fields. Detroit was the fifth largest city in America, and Cleveland was the sixth. The economy of the Ohio city was more diversified, but it was also a major player in the auto industry. They were only 190 miles apart and were linked by overnight boat service across Lake Erie.

The Indians and Tigers delighted in knocking each other out of pennant races. When Bob Feller faced Hal Newhouser in the American League's greatest pitching matchup, the two stadiums were packed. The Tigers had taunted the Indians as "crybabies" and hung diapers in their dugout when they beat Cleveland out of the 1940 pennant. The Indians paid them back 10 years later, beating the Tigers twice in the season's final week to give the pennant to the Yankees.

And then there was that Ohio State–Michigan thing.

So this rivalry had a long pedigree.

The Cleveland Browns and the Detroit Lions had met only once before, earlier in the 1952 season, at Briggs Stadium. The Lions won 17–6.

This had not been a great season for the Browns. They were only 8–4, losing twice, to the Giants and to the Eagles, as well as Detroit. The season-ending loss to the Giants had been brutal. Speedie and Dub Jones were out of the title game with injuries, and Groza, who had broken ribs, was only available for kicking.

Brown was more concerned with team attitude. The team had won five championships and six division titles in the last six years. Many of the veterans wanted to know why their salaries didn't reflect that level of achievement. They understood that their careers were nearing the end and were concerned about their futures.

Graham took the position that playoff money was practically guaranteed in a contract with the Browns, so that should be considered as part of the base salary. But he was also the highest-paid member of the team.

The players had voted to exclude the assistant coaches and clubhouse personnel from the 1952 playoff money. Brown was deeply disappointed in them and insisted that the front office make up their share.

He felt betrayed when Speedie jumped to Canada after this season, and the two men didn't speak for the next 25 years.

So the Browns went into the title game with serious problems both on and off the field. In addition to that, Brown had lost confidence in his team. After all, hadn't they shown that they were just playing for the paychecks, the thing he always had warned them against? In the Lions he saw a hungry team, the way the Browns used to be. The Lions were made 3-point favorites. Brown said it should be 17, even though the game was to be played in Cleveland.

To many in the Detroit organization, this sounded like a con job. "More Paul Brown propaganda," said the team's offensive line coach, Aldo Forte. "I'd call him an honest man with deceiving ways."

The Detroit papers speculated that Brown was "keeping his movie machine whirring overtime" in his plans to upend the upstarts.

But there was no secret plan. The Lions methodically defeated the Browns, 17–7. Groza missed three field goals. Graham outpassed Layne but couldn't connect when it counted. With the Browns driving to tie the game in the third quarter, Motley was thrown for a five-yard loss near the goal line. Walker broke loose on a 67-yard run to score his only touchdown of the season.

"It takes inspiration to win the title," said Bert Bell tellingly, while praising Detroit as "possibly the best team the pro game has ever seen."

The NFL still had not forgiven Brown for showing it up two years prior. This defeat had been deeply satisfying for the league's old guard. They didn't mind at all that a bunch of roisterers had won the title. Isn't that how their game used to be before Brown came in and took all the fun out of it, with his notebooks and movies and organization?

Brown came away from the season realizing that the Browns were in trouble. If they wanted to stay on top, it was time for changes.

The NFL's first venture into Texas ended in total disaster in 1952. The Dallas Texans were broke by midseason. The league had to step in to operate the team, and at the end of the year the team's assets were transferred to a new edition of the Baltimore Colts.

The former Colts had died an ignominious death after 1950, their only season in the NFL. They had transferred with Cleveland and San Francisco from the old AAFC and became the only one of the three to fail.

New owner Carroll Rosenbloom felt the team needed immediate credibility to make up for the failures of the recent past. So in January 1953, he and Brown engineered one of the biggest trades in the history of the league. The Browns sent 10 players to Baltimore, including the man who one day would be their coach, Don Shula. In return, Cleveland got its rebuilding done in a hurry.

Mike McCormack would become an All-Pro on the Brown's offensive line, Don Colo stepped in at defensive tackle, and Tom Catlin shored up the linebackers. All three would go on to become team captains. More than that, Brown felt they were all hungry. They hadn't been spoiled by success.

The top draft choice, Doug Atkins, moved right in at end opposite Ford. The versatile Ray Renfro led the team in rushing and was second to Dante Lavelli in receiving. The defensive backfield, headed by Warren Lahr, was deadly, picking off 25 opposition passes.

The Browns once again had the lean and mean players their coach liked so much.

Five months later, McBride sold the team. A syndicate headed by local businessman David Jones bought the Browns for $600,000.

Brown was furious that the deal was completed without his knowledge. He was told later that McBride thought the team was on a downward slope and decided to get out while the getting was good.

Brown was equally incensed at what he felt was an insultingly low sales price. As a shareholder, this hurt him in the wallet. The new owners assured him they would honor all contractual agreements made with McBride. They also said they were content to stay in the deep background and let Brown run things as he saw fit. He was somewhat mollified but never spoke to McBride again.

Whatever the reason, the Browns seemed to be their old selves again in the 1953 season. They won their first 11 games in a row, stumbling only in a meaningless finale against Philadelphia. The defense held the opposition to an average of fewer than 14 points per game, while Cleveland was scoring 29 per game on average. They even managed to sell out the big stadium for the first time in the NFL, as 81,000 turned out to watch the 49ers go down 23-21.

But the Lions had come back with an equally formidable team. They finished 10-2, losing only to the Rams twice.

And so the Lions and the Browns met up for the championship game. This time, however, it was a Detroit player who had the critical injury. Leon Hart, who played what would later be called tight end, had to leave the game. He was the team's leading receiver, and in his place Parker inserted a defensive end, Jim Doran, who had put in almost no time with the offense all year. Against the league's top pass defense, it seemed like an odd decision.

The Lions were as rowdy as ever. The team had been accused of playing dirty against San Francisco, deliberately kneeing Tittle in the back. Three Detroit players reportedly got into a fight with some 49ers fans outside a restaurant after the game. The players won.

The 49ers had small reason to complain, though. In the game at Cleveland, Graham had been thrown out of bounds and then punched in the mouth by one of the San Francisco linebackers. Graham had to leave the game but came back in the second half to key the Browns' victory.

The incident stirred Brown's memories of Len Ford's career-threatening facial injury three years prior. Pro football has always been a rough game, and injuries are regarded as an occupational hazard. In the current version of the sport, however, most injuries are the result of collisions between 300-pound linemen moving with the speed of sprinters and normal human beings. Or when the big men get tangled in a pileup and start falling over each other.

In the game of the 1950s, though, the mayhem was more calculated. The Eagles' defensive front, nicknamed the "Suicide Seven," was notorious for such bashing in the trenches. The Lions' defensive back Jimmy David wasn't called "the Hatchet" because he was an avid woodsman. The field was a war zone.

Graham's injury prompted Brown to consult with the Riddell Company, which marketed the first plastic helmets. They devised a tubular bar that ran across the mouth area. Previous designs had used a bar of Lucite, but it shattered at hard impact and the league banned its use. The new version, called the BT-5 (for Bar Tubular and the fifth attempt at making it work), was a combination of plastic and rubber. It was ready for the 1955 season, and Graham was the first player to wear it.

Within a year, it had been adopted by most players, and another bar was added to protect the nose. The last man to eschew the bar was

Layne, who continued playing with his bare face showing until his retirement in 1962. Washington quarterback Bill Kilmer was the last quarterback to use only the single bar, according to the *NFL Encyclopedia*. Brown didn't much like the sort of play that led to a need for such a device. Truth be told, he didn't much like the Lions. He admired Parker as a coach, and their two staffs had a cordial relationship, even going on golf outings during the off-season. But way down deep, the behavior of Parker's team, and especially Layne, offended Brown's belief about what football should stand for. He wanted this 1953 title game as much as he'd wanted any.

It turned out to be one of the bitterest defeats he ever had known.

Graham was off his game. An early fumble led to Detroit's only touchdown in the first half. An interception led to a field goal. Graham completed only two passes all day, for a total of 20 yards.

He explained later that his hands were chapped, and he had no feel on his passes. "I tried spitting on them, everything I could think of to moisten them," he said. "I had no idea what the matter was, but I just could not pass on that day."

Eventually, he asked Brown to let him come out of the game for a while. The coach knew that something had to be terribly wrong for Graham to make such a request. Brown put his backup, George Ratterman, in the game, but Ratterman couldn't move the Browns either.

Still, the Browns trailed only 10–3 at the half. When Graham came back he was able to get Cleveland close enough for three Groza field goals. "The Toe" had become one of the most feared weapons in the league. He made 23 out of 26 field-goal attempts during the year and scored 108 points, almost one-third of the Cleveland total. Around the league, it was said that when you played Cleveland you had to treat the 30-yard line as the goal line. Closer than that and Groza was deadly.

His third field goal gave the Browns a 16–10 lead with a bit more than four minutes to go. What happened next became a legend in Detroit and a misery in Cleveland.

Doak Walker, speaking 33 years later at the funeral of his lifelong friend, said, "Bobby Layne never lost a game in his life. Time just ran out on him."

It didn't on this day. With a sold-out Briggs Stadium roaring and the ball at his own 20, Layne went into the huddle and said: "Just give me some time and block for me, boys, and I'll win you a title." At least, that's the sanitized version. There are as many accounts of what Layne actually said as there are of Babe Ruth's called-shot home run in the 1932 World Series.

But for one of the few times during the day, the Lions started to move. Layne was finding Doran on critical plays, one for 17 yards and another for 18. The end was engaged in a vicious personal battle with Lahr, the two men bumping and scratching at each other on every down. Doran had thrown an elbow at him earlier, and Lahr took affront.

Layne was observing this carefully and so was assistant coach Aldo Forte up in the press box. In two minutes, the Lions had moved to the Cleveland 33 and called a timeout. They were down by six and needed a touchdown to win.

Ford was putting tremendous pressure on the Detroit quarterback, and it was suggested that a screen pass might work. But Layne had watched Lahr wagging a finger at Doran and yelling something after the previous play. Layne was a poker player and a serious student of human nature. He knew that angry men often make bad decisions.

"You know what I think," he said on the sidelines. "I think a cigarette would taste real good right now."

With that he trotted back into the huddle and called the play. Doran was to go out, hesitate as if still on the curl pattern he had been running, and then break downfield. Doran said later he thought Lahr was going to knock his head off when he came at him after the snap.

Doran shot past him unencumbered and gathered in Layne's pass for the touchdown. It was the only one he would score all year—just as

Walker's decisive 67-yard run in the 1952 game had been his only touchdown of the year.

Still, there were two minutes left, and Graham had been in this place before. In the 1950 game, trailing by one point, he had driven the Browns to a Groza field goal and the championship. Now he just needed to reach the Detroit 30, after all.

Not this time. Graham still could not make his passes behave, and when Carl Karilivacz intercepted the first fluttering ball he threw, Cleveland was dead.

The train ride home was funereal.

"This one stuck in the gut," said Groza.

Brown, as always, gathered himself and called it "heartbreaking," which may have emphasized his gift for understatement.

Lahr sat by himself in the coach, refusing to speak or to be consoled. Brown said he never felt worse for anyone in his life. He was taking the game entirely on his shoulders after contributing so much during the season. A few days later, Brown took Lahr aside, told him, "Don't let this destroy you," and quietly gave him a raise for the 1954 season.

Upon arriving at training camp the next summer, Graham announced that the upcoming season would be his last. It was the inevitability that Brown had been dreading.

The quarterback had been the perfect extension of the coach's mind for eight seasons, executing the game plans as flawlessly as they had been conceived. More than that, he had the one essential gift: he knew how to win.

"There is only one way to judge a quarterback," Brown said, "and that is by wins and losses. By that measure, Graham was the greatest ever to play the game."

It's hard to argue with that. His record in all regular- and postseason games, in both the NFL and AAFC, was 105-17-4.

Graham occasionally had a bad game. But he never had a bad year. His consistency was astonishing. Every season in the NFL he would attempt approximately 260 passes and complete approximately 145 of them. In 1952 he threw more because the team had no running game. In 1955 he threw less, but every other year, he hit those averages almost exactly.

One hundred seventy-four of those passes went for touchdowns. One-third of all Cleveland's points during his career came from his passes. That would be hard to replace, and Brown knew it only too well. But the performance came with a price, and Graham had taken a terrific physical pounding. The smash-mouth thing with the 49ers was only the most severe. He'd had enough.

His backup since 1952 was Ratterman. Once more it was a case of Brown admiring an opponent and then getting him. Ratterman had led a fairly ragtag Buffalo Bills team into the AAFC playoffs against Cleveland in 1948 and 1949. While he never beat the Browns, he did tie them twice, and the coach was taken by the effort.

Ratterman had thrown 52 touchdown passes in that league but also held the record of 55 interceptions, too. Brown felt that with the proper control he would be an admirable backup. Besides, he was an Ohio boy from St. Xavier High School in Cincinnati.

Ratterman was used to the role. He had spent his college career backing up All-American Johnny Lujack at Notre Dame. Only a surprise performance in the 1947 College All-Star Game, in which he led the collegians to an upset of the Bears, put him on the charts at all.

Brown eventually rescued him from the same dreadful New York Yankees organization that had coughed up Layne. Ratterman had many of the same attributes. A practical joker, his forte was inserting hot powder in the jock straps of his teammates. While on another team, he called the switchboard of the hotel where the Browns were staying and told the operator to let the players know that practice had been cancelled because of rain. It hadn't been, and the Browns should have known better. Brown would have cancelled for a typhoon, maybe. Never for mere rain.

But Ratterman's finest moment came when Brown sent in one of his messenger guards with a play. Ratterman listened, and then told the messenger, "Go back there and tell Paul I want to run something else." The guard stood there goggle-eyed until he was reassured that Ratterman was only kidding. No one would dare take that sort of message back to Brown.

In those days, starting quarterbacks actually came out of games when things weren't going well. A coach who tried that today would have a princely sulk on his hands for weeks and controversy in the newspapers for a month. But in the 1950s it was understood that every so often a quarterback needed to sit out for a quarter to clear his head and see how things looked from the sidelines. Graham and Layne did it, and frequently they would reenter the game in the second half and get the win. Different times, different customs.

On those instances when Ratterman replaced Graham, he didn't do badly at all. In 1953 he played in nine of the 12 games and threw for four touchdowns.

Brown also knew that playing as a backup was a much different thing than being the starter. He had made up his mind that Ratterman wasn't the long-term answer. But draft choices at the position hadn't worked out either. So the new season began with a sense of closing.

The G-men—Groza, Gatski, and Abe Gibron—still held down the offensive line. Speedie was gone, but Lavelli and Jones were back as receivers. Willis had retired, but McCormack was moved into the middle guard post. And Ford and James were also returning on defense.

The Browns were being remade on the fly. Chuck Noll, who would also go on to some considerable coaching success, was now one of the messenger guards. Maurice Bassett was becoming a serviceable replacement for Motley, who had to sit out the year with an injury, at fullback.

The team stumbled out of the gate, losing badly to Philadelphia and getting blasted, shockingly, by the Steelers, 55–27. Much of this was caused by transition in the coaching staff. Two of Brown's longtime assistants, Blanton Collier and Weeb Ewbank, were gone to head coaching jobs: Collier to the University of Kentucky and Ewbank to the Colts. It took a while to adjust.

Brown was glad to see his old friend Collier land the job. But Ewbank's departure was not altogether friendly. Ewbank was one of the principal architects of Cleveland's 1954 draft plans. Brown insisted that he stay with the team until after draft day, and Commissioner Bell agreed. As it turned out, this was not in Cleveland's best interest. Loyalty is one thing, but it was unreasonable to suppose that Ewbank would pick against the best interests of his own future.

Players who Brown knew were on his team's list for the lower rounds started getting picked off by the Colts before he could get at them. The most telling example was Ray Berry. He had not made anyone's head turn as an end at Southern Methodist, but he'd impressed Brown with his uncanny ability to run sideline patterns. But Baltimore snapped him up, and Brown was keenly perturbed.

It turned out that Ewbank, while seated at the Cleveland desk, was surreptitiously passing selection notes to Baltimore sportswriter John Steadman, who then carried them to the Colts. That's a good example of how journalistic ethics codes have changed a lot since 1954.

Ewbank had promised the Colts organization a winner within five years. Berry was a major element in enabling him to beat that timetable by one season.

The Browns managed to right themselves after the early drubbing in Pittsburgh and were soon running with accustomed precision once more. They would not lose again, in fact, until the final game of the season. The opponents were the Detroit Lions.

The game meant nothing. Both teams already had clinched their divisions and would meet for the third straight year for the championship the following Sunday.

It had been scheduled as an October game, but events dictated otherwise. Cleveland had gone agog over the Indians, who were on their way to a league-record 111 victories for the year. The original date of the Lions-Browns meeting at Cleveland Stadium was preempted by the World Series.

Hopes for a repeat of 1948, when both Cleveland teams had won championships, were quickly dashed. The underdog New York Giants stunned baseball with a four-game sweep of the Series.

The city was crushed, and now here were the Browns coming up against the team and coach that had handled them every time they met. For the first time since he lost the first three games he coached against Canton McKinley, Brown was hearing the word *jinx*. Some people were saying even worse—that he was being consistently outcoached by Parker. Moreover, some of the same opinion was coming from Brown's own players.

The season-ending game may have been meaningless, but Cleveland fans wanted a statement, some indication that the Browns could prevail against these Lions. After three straight title-game losses, one to the Rams and twice to Detroit, attendance had dipped to disappointing lows. The Browns were barely averaging 30,000 fans per game. Maybe McBride had been right to bail out. With Graham set to retire and the Browns apparently heading for another beat-down by the Lions, the franchise did seem to be on the downward slope.

Cleveland's performance in the 14-10 loss in the season's last game did little to allay these fears.

It was a cold, snowy day, and Brown decided to go conservative once more. Conservative may be an exaggeration. Graham threw just six passes and completed one of them for a grand total of four yards.

Layne, meanwhile, was flinging the football all over the yard. In the last two and a half minutes, in a drive disturbingly reminiscent of the previous December's title game, he moved the Lions 75 yards for a touchdown and the win. The pass was once again thrown over Lahr.

"We never seem to have much luck against Detroit," shrugged Brown. "We try to get a little more information about the Lions than any of the other clubs. So far, it hasn't seemed to help.

"We tried to sit on a lead and failed, but it was the kind of game to play in that kind of weather. I would play it the same way all over again. We made a few mistakes. I hope they won't be repeated."

Fans in both Cleveland and Detroit were dumbfounded. How could he take such a casual attitude at getting thumped again, for the fourth straight time, by Detroit?

It was billed as a nothing game, "but the players went at each other to the hilt," noted *The Detroit News*. "Unquestionably, Brown must change his tactics. What will he do to counter Detroit's psychological advantage? Brown is in peril of becoming the most unsuccessful coach in playoff history. With another loss to the Lions he stands to lose personal prestige, and so does Graham."

The *Detroit Free Press*, meanwhile, headlined its account of the game "Nothing Fazes Lions Now." Even Parker's postgame warning—"This can't go on forever"—didn't dampen spirits in Detroit. Or among the oddsmakers. They installed the Lions as two-and-a-half-point favorites for the following Sunday's repeat of the game on the same field.

The Cleveland papers, meanwhile, blasted Brown's play-calling. There was also a secret meeting of several Cleveland players. They agreed that if they fell behind to the Lions again they would simply ignore Brown's plays and open up the offense. The team seemed close to an open mutiny.

If there was method in Brown's tactics he never let on, either in statements after the game or in words written years later. He knew the frustration that was boiling up on his team at its inability to beat the Lions. He also knew how badly they wanted to win this last game for Graham. Brown just let it all lie there for the week; he let the Browns think about it.

Cleveland was distracted briefly when the verdict came in on the Dr. Sam Sheppard trial the day after the loss to the Lions. It was the most sensational case of its time and had transfixed the city for months. The successful local dentist who was accused of murdering his wife was the basis for *The Fugitive* television series and the more recent movie of the same name. Sheppard was convicted, and debates over his guilt continued for decades. (The conviction was eventually reversed, and Sheppard was acquitted in a second trial.)

But by the end of the week, the Browns were back as Topic A. Almost 44,000 fans came to the stadium, the biggest crowd of the season, to see if the Browns could dispel the dark cloud that had settled over the city.

Did they ever. In the most decisive title game since the Bears had run up 73 on Washington in 1940, the Browns smoked Detroit, 56–10.

All the built-up emotions were let loose on the Lions, who reacted as if the punching bag had suddenly grown fists and hit back. The Browns intercepted six passes and recovered three fumbles. Every time the Lions gave a hint of getting back into the game they were smacked down again.

It was 35–10 at the half, and just to extinguish all hope, the Browns rolled for two more touchdowns at the start of the third quarter.

The Cleveland papers noted impishly that the Lions had stopped Groza from kicking a field goal. His services weren't required this time.

Graham was brilliant, playing as if this were personal vindication against the team that thwarted him so often. He had never thrown a touchdown pass in a game with Detroit. He threw for three touchdowns this time and ran for three more.

"We beat a good team having a bad day," said Brown. "The same thing has happened to me, and it could happen to anyone. A coach lives in dread of a day like this and knows he can avoid it only so long. But I told my kids that on this day they were the finest team I ever had."

The news photos show Brown leaving the field, right fist upraised in the long-delayed triumph.

Layne waved off speculation that the Lions had taken the Browns too lightly. He said that he had been on his best behavior. He knew the history. If the Lions had won, they would have been the first team ever in pro football to take three titles in a row. That would have been nice.

"I went to bed at 10:00 PM the night before," he said, "and we got the devil beat out of us. I know I was awful. I never felt right."

Parker accepted Layne's explanation with a wry grin.

"I guess when a kid's been used to having a drink since he was 14, you don't want to change his habits. Our luck just ran out. We never had so many things go against us so fast."

The Lions pointed to all sorts of bad breaks in the early going, breaks that might have changed the momentum. But no one who saw this game thought that the Browns could have been stopped by anything. Not on this day.

In the euphoria of the Browns locker room, however, there was a sudden reminder of what it was they had just witnessed.

"After this, I'm through," Graham affirmed. "It's the Pro Bowl, and then I'm retired."

For the first time in their history, the Browns looked ahead to a new season with doubt. Their leader had left the building.

12

1955: Cleveland Browns 38, Los Angeles Rams 14

Then, again, maybe their leader hadn't really left.

Otto Graham was dedicated to Paul Brown and his system. But there were times when even he was taken aback at the coach's increasingly arbitrary methods. Graham bristled most at the ubiquitous messenger guards. He felt he was fully capable of calling his own plays. While he did have the discretion to check off at the line of scrimmage and call another play, he better have a good explanation for doing it—at least, if it didn't work. If it did, nothing was said.

Graham was tired mentally as well as physically. Although Brown said he was trying to relieve his quarterback of stress by sending in the plays, that system took a toll on an individual with a leader's mentality.

Nine years was enough. Graham was just 33 years old. In the current scheme of things, he'd be regarded as in his prime as a quarterback. John Elway won two Super Bowls with the Denver Broncos after turning 37. But in 1954, 33 was a ripe old age in football terms. Graham meant his retirement seriously and fully intended to make it stick.

Of course, the question then is why did he agree to have dinner with Brown just three days after Cleveland lost the College All-Star Game in August 1955?

The All-Star game had raised some questions in the coach. Brown, always sensing conspiracies against his success, accused the game's sponsors of letting the Soldier Field grass grow too high in order to hinder Lou Groza's kicking. Brown overlooked the fact that the All-Stars had won on a field goal. But Brown never let the facts get in the way of a good theory.

But beyond the height of the grass, Brown sensed that something wasn't right with his team. It just didn't feel like the Cleveland Browns out on the practice field. The more he saw of George Ratterman's skills as a ball handler, scrambler, and field leader, the more Brown felt the need to get one more year out of Graham. Then Brown would take his chances again in the draft.

Meanwhile, Brown was tinkering with the offense in order to make it easier for his quarterback to return. In a sharp departure from recent years, Cleveland would be a team almost evenly balanced between running and passing in 1955. The previous season the Browns had passed for over 500 yards more than they ran, and in 1953 they had gained almost twice as many yards passing as running. But this time around the gap would be cut to fewer than 200 yards.

Brown brought in Ed Modzelewski, a big punishing runner, in a trade with Pittsburgh and teamed him with Fred Morrison. The two backs combined for 1,443 yards in 1955. The ageless Dante Lavelli, with the best hands in the game, would still be around to throw to. The versatile Mike McCormack was switched back from middle guard to offensive tackle to expedite the running game. Chuck Noll went the other way, moving from guard to outside linebacker.

The 1955 team was Brown at his best: always looking for the new approach, searching for the more effective way of getting it done. It was enough to convince Graham. That, and a contract for $25,000, the biggest in the league.

Ironically, however, in working so hard to coax Graham back for one more year, Brown had unwittingly surrendered the future. A young quarterback who had been cut by Pittsburgh sent a telegram to Brown requesting a tryout. Although this player hadn't been drafted by the Steelers until the ninth round, Brown had heard positive things about him. But with Graham coming back there was no room left on the roster.

Brown did respond, asking him to hold it together until the following summer, when he would do his best to get him an invitation to training camp. But while playing semipro football in the Pittsburgh area, the quarterback got a call from the Colts, who offered a far more substantial invitation.

Which is why Cleveland would go on searching fruitlessly for Graham's successor, while Johnny Unitas ended up in Baltimore.

Ratterman replaced Graham during the second half of the opener, a loss to Washington. Then the Browns went 9–1–1 just like old times, as if Graham had never considered leaving.

The Browns were tops in the league in offense, number one in defense, crushing opponents on most Sundays. The Browns even managed to kick up attendance a bit, to almost 45,000 a game. But on the final Sunday, with Graham playing his last game in Cleveland—and this time for sure—the crowd was only 26,000.

Their former stumbling block, the Lions, never seemed to recover from the previous December's thrashing. They plunged all the way to the bottom of the NFL West, with a 3–9 record. "Sooner or later it has to happen to every coach," said Buddy Parker, "unless his name is Paul Brown."

Instead, it was the Browns' earlier sparring partner, the Los Angeles Rams, who showed up in December. But even their most ardent supporters knew that this wasn't an especially good team. The runners-up in the conference, the Bears, had handled them twice rather easily.

Under first-year coach Sid Gillman, the Rams ran the ball better than they used to. Ron Waller and Tank Younger were almost as effective as the Browns' running tandem, gaining 1,360 yards. The defense had improved, too, with linebacker Les Richter and end Andy Robustelli keying it.

But some things don't change, and the Rams were still essentially a passing show. Norm Van Brocklin was not at his peak, throwing almost twice as many interceptions as touchdowns. But even a lesser Van Brocklin was a Pro Bowl quarterback, and he still had Tom Fears, Elroy Hirsch, and Bob Boyd on the receiving end.

On the seven-and-a-half-hour flight into Los Angeles, the Browns were a confident bunch. They were six-and-a-half-points favorites, and no one disputed the spread. There was no reason to.

The Browns won going away. Gillman thought he could stop the Browns' passing with a zone defense, but Graham figured it out in a hurry. By the half, it was 17–7 for Cleveland. When the Rams switched back to man-to-man coverage in the second half, Graham picked them apart. He hit Lavelli on a 50-yard touchdown pass and Ray Renfro for 35 more, and then he ran for two himself.

Meanwhile, Van Brocklin was smothered, threw six interceptions, and was finally benched in favor of Bill Wade, who could do no better.

While not quite as furious as the destruction of Detroit a year before, it was a convincing show of superiority. The Browns once again were kings of football and Graham the greatest in the game. Each of the winning players received $3,508. (The winners of the 2005 Super Bowl made $68,000 apiece.)

"Never before has one player so dominated," wrote the *Chicago Tribune*, a tribute echoed by every pro football writer. "There may have been greater runners. Graham has faced rivals who were superlative forward passers. But no man has combined these skills with his intellectual mastery of the precepts of the 'T' attack."

One of the New York papers, somewhat more cynically (naturally), labeled it "Otto Graham's Annual Farewell Game."

But this was for keeps. "Nothing would induce me to come back again," he said. "It's been a grand and glorious 10 years." Brown knew it was futile to try and change his mind one more time.

There was nothing left to prove. He had done it all.

"Graham and Brown Firm Dissolution Marks End of Era in Pro Football," said the headline in the hometown *The Plain Dealer*.

But not really the end. Surely not. After all, the Browns' revised running attack was the best in the league.

"Defense will carry the Browns through," wrote columnist Gordon Cobbledick. "The bell will ring, and the Browns will be there. They won't fall apart because a great player has hung 'em up for keeps. The greatest line in pro football will be back.

"And so will Paul Brown."

But, as it must for all men, the reckoning came for Brown, in 1956.

He had been coaching for a quarter of a century. He began as the country was entering the Great Depression; leading hungry young men with fire, but not much food, in their bellies to greater successes than they ever had dreamed of. He continued through the war, when character was tested as never before. He knew the boys he coached. He understood their background, the way they'd grown up, the music that made them dance. He liked 'em lean and mean, and he liked Ohio boys, just as he had been. But the old order changes, and the team he had hand-picked so meticulously was just about gone.

If, when the Browns left the field at the Los Angeles Coliseum in December 1955, anyone had written that it was the last championship Paul Brown would ever win, the words would have been greeted with chortles of disbelief. His team was still at its peak, purring along as it always had.

But the motor was a 1946 model, and it had run as far as it could go.

And the coach was now 48 years old, no longer the boy wonder of Massillon and Columbus. The ground was shifting beneath his feet, and the old answers were still being given to altogether different questions.

In the spring of 1955, McDonald's opened its first outlet. A couple of months later, Disneyland opened its doors. In the summer, "Rock Around the Clock" became the first rock 'n' roll song to reach number one on the Hit Parade. The nation was in the full tide of postwar prosperity. Moms were joining the work force, and fast food provided more and more family meals. There was money for vacations and trips to theme parks. The older values—sacrifice, delayed gratification, dedication to the rules, home, family—were slowly fading away.

Brown had become a big band kind of guy in a rock 'n' roll world. The words were unfamiliar, and the beat was all wrong.

Buddy Parker's tribute of the previous year proved false in 1956. The bottom can drop out, even if your name is Paul Brown.

Brown brought in Tommy O'Connell and Babe Parilli to back up Ratterman. But it just didn't work. Parilli would go on to lead the Boston Patriots to a divisional title in the new American Football League in a few more years, but he never bought into Brown's system and was sent back to Green Bay, from whence he had come, after one year.

O'Connell was more willing and an adept student of the high-percentage passing game Brown favored. But the spark of leadership wasn't there. Ratterman, who had waited for this chance for so long, went down with an injury and only got into four games all year. The Browns ended up gaining more yards running than they did passing.

The defense did show up as scheduled, and once again it was the best in the NFL. But the Cleveland offense ranked 11th of the 12 teams.

The Browns were in almost every game they played. Nobody was blowing them out. And in the next-to-last game of the regular season they went into New York and knocked off the Giants, who would win the NFL title, 24-7. But that was the Browns' highest point total of the season, and they could never recover from an unprecedented three straight losses early in the season. They finished 5-7.

Not since 1943 and the Baby Bucks of Ohio State University had Brown gone through a losing season. But that had been an aberration, a result of wartime exigencies beyond his control. This time, Brown knew that for a half dozen or so plays over the course of the season, the final result could have been reversed, or even better. The fate of the Browns was still in his hands, and in 1957 he set out to make them over once and for all. The engine for doing that would be the draft.

He knew what he needed: a quarterback. There were several good ones coming out of college: John Brodie from Stanford University, Paul Hornung from Notre Dame University, and Len Dawson from Purdue University. But Brodie and Hornung were the first two players drafted, and it came down to a coin flip between the Browns and Pittsburgh over who would get Dawson. The Steelers won.

Dawson eventually would win a championship, but it was with the Kansas City Chiefs. Hornung would win several, but as a running back at Green Bay. Brodie would go on to several great years with the non-contending 49ers.

With those three top quarterbacks gone, the Browns settled on the best player left on the board. They chose Jim Brown of Syracuse University.

They got the greatest running back in the history of football. But it turned out to be a case of one Brown too many for the Browns, and the eventual undoing of their coach.

13

Decline and Fall

There are stars, and then there are superstars.

The Browns had been a team filled with stars, led by a superstar quarterback in Otto Graham. He was the best of his era.

Jim Brown was the new superstar.

He arrived in Cleveland just as television was remaking the landscape of professional football. It was no longer a Sunday diversion from the sports that really mattered, baseball and college football. The NFL was about to become the biggest game in town.

Its personalities were larger than life. Every game was an epic struggle. It was the first of all the professional sports to become an adjunct of show business. It was must-see TV.

Television demanded superstars who more than merely players. They were also supposed to be celebrities. Jim Brown filled the bill. He was an incredibly handsome man, along with being a charismatic athlete. Pro football had seen great runners before. The game had been built on the legs of Jim Thorpe, Red Grange, Bronko Nagurski. But none could remember a runner with such a complete package of power and speed. If Brown couldn't run away from you, he'd run right over you.

"For mercurial speed, airy nimbleness, and explosive violence in one package of evil, there is no other like Mr. Brown," wrote the great sports journalist Red Smith, who had seen most of them come and go.

Writer James Toback, who knew the running back in later years, claimed that "Brown did more than any other man to originate what became a national obsession with the game. He was a consistent and spectacular warrior, the embodiment of his team, a crystalization of physical potency. He gave a new dimension to the sport as its first black hero."

That may be overstating it somewhat, but you get the idea.

Brown was raised on Long Island, New York, and at Manhasset High School won 13 letters for basketball, baseball, lacrosse, and track, as well as football. When he went to Syracuse University, he continued to star on the basketball team and was an All-American in lacrosse. But he became a national figure in football. As a senior he rushed for nearly 1,000 yards in an eight-game season—more than 120 yards per game. He scored 43 points in one game against Colgate University and then went on to score three touchdowns in the nationally televised Cotton Bowl.

By the time he joined the Browns he was 6'2" and 230 pounds; this was at a time when 250 pounds was considered big for a defensive lineman.

Opponents marveled at the way he could hold the entire field in his range of vision, how he could make his leg go slack and then drive away from a tackler who was convinced that he had Brown within his grasp.

Giants middle linebacker Sam Huff gave the classic answer when asked what the best way was to stop Brown.

"Mug him on the way out of the locker room," said Huff.

But if it was tough on linemen and linebackers to stop him, it was a nightmare for smaller defensive backs. Charlie Jackson, who played for the Cardinals in those years, recalled what it was like in a 1999 interview with *The Sporting News*.

"It was an awful sensation when Brown came blowin' through the hole and right at you," he said. "You felt like you were trapped on a trestle by an unscheduled freight train."

Coach Brown didn't hesitate to put the back in the starting lineup immediately. "When you have a Thoroughbred, you run him," he said.

Not that he didn't see imperfections in the young man's game. The player wasn't too keen on blocking, and to the coach that was a major flaw. Coach Brown's offensive system had been based on the fullback, originally Motley, staying in to protect the quarterback. The coach also

Paul Brown, right, and quarterback Otto Graham, center, are shown in the dressing room in Cleveland on December 27, 1954, after the Browns upended the Detroit Lions 56–10 in the NFL title game. At left is Graham's father.

A referee raises his arms to signal a touchdown as American professional football player Otto Graham kneels in the end zone during a game between the New York Giants and Cleveland Browns, 1956. Also involved in the play was no. 76 Lou Groza, tackle and placekicker for the Cleveland Browns.

Cleveland Browns Hall of Fame head coach Paul Brown in 1962, his last year with the team.

Cincinnati Bengals quarterback Greg Cook (left), posing with other players at a banquet at the Kentucky Touchdown Club.

Greg Cook during an AFL football game.

Cincinnati Bengals rookie quarterback Greg Cook (no. 12) talks to head coach Paul Brown between offensive series during a 40–7 loss to the New York Jets on November 23, 1969, at Shea Stadium in Flushing, New York.

Cincinnati Bengals coach Paul Brown operates a movie projector beside which he spent many hours each week going over films of the Bengal's and their opponents. He was named the Associated Press Coach of the Year of the AFL in Cincinnati on December 11, 1969. Brown, one of football's most successful coaches, was a stickler for fundamentals and precision.
AP PHOTO/HARVEY EUGENE SMITH

Defensive end Royce Berry, no. 82 of the Cincinnati Bengals, looks to shed the block of center Fred Hoaglin, no. 54 of the Cleveland Browns during a game on October 11, 1970 at Municipal Stadium in Cleveland, Ohio. PHOTO BY: TONY TOMSIC/GETTY IMAGES

Cincinnati Bengals Hall of Fame head coach Paul Brown circa the early-1970s.

Cincinnati Bengals quarterback Virgil Carter (no. 11) barks signals while center Bob Johnson (no. 54) waits to snap the ball during a 15–12 loss to the Los Angeles Rams on October 22, 1972, at the Los Angeles Memorial Coliseum in Los Angeles, California.

Quarterback Ken Anderson (no. 14) of the Cincinnati Bengals looks for an open receiver during a 27–22 loss to the Kansas City Chiefs on September 9, 1984. During the game, Anderson surpassed 25,000 passing yards for his career. PHOTO BY VIC MILTON/NFL

Cincinnati Bengals owner Mike Brown—shown standing with his father and Bengals founder, Paul Brown, right, during practice at Spinney Field in Cincinnati, December 12, 1986—made an agreement with Hamilton County officials to name the Bengals new stadium after his father. AP PHOTO/AL BEHRMAN

Paul Brown Stadium, where the Cincinnati Bengals play, is shown in this, April 1, 2004, photo.

felt that his new running back wasn't carrying his weight in blocking for other runners.

"He got miffed at me one day when I told him he was graded last among all our running backs as a blocker," said the coach in his autobiography, *PB*. "But then I backed up the grades with some film clips. He said nothing, but I knew he resented the criticism."

In his rookie year, Jim Brown rushed for 942 yards, led the league, and restored the Browns to the championship game. It was the lowest rushing total he would amass over the next eight years, when he led the NFL seven times. He never missed a single game.

The entire city felt the excitement of this new force. The crowds came out to see this incredible new player. The Browns averaged more than 50,000 at the gate for the first time since leaving the AAFC.

With 65,000 in the house for the game against the Rams, Brown had his greatest day yet. He broke the NFL rushing record with 237 yards and scored four touchdowns in the 45–31 rout.

What made this all the more remarkable is that Brown's performance seemed to inspire O'Connell. The journeyman quarterback had his best season as a pro. With Renfro and Darrel Brewster as his primary targets, and defenses stacked to stop Brown, O'Connell gave Cleveland a dangerous passing attack once more. But when he went down with an ankle injury late in the year, the Browns had to turn to plan B. This was the quarterback they had made their second-round pick in the draft: Milt Plum.

The Browns knew they had missed out on the top of the class. The report on Plum at Penn State was "no frills, competent." The coach never warmed to him throughout his entire stay in Cleveland and said candidly that the only thing standing between the Browns and more championships was their quarterback.

"He refused to stay within his limitations and work with the offense we prepared for him," wrote Brown in his autobiography. "Milt really was a nice man, but not cut out to be a leader."

O'Connell would be ready to play in the championship game. But he was still not fully mobile, and Plum was also hobbled with a pulled hamstring.

⚭ • ⚭

The Browns' championship opponents once more would be the Detroit Lions. They had come from deep in the pack at the end of the season to force a playoff game with San Francisco. Then they came from three touchdowns behind in the second half to pull that one out.

But the equation had changed in Detroit over a long, strange season. On the eve of the opener, Coach Buddy Parker had stood up at the team banquet in a downtown hotel and, without any previous warning, quit right on the spot.

The audience thought he was kidding, and even the master of ceremonies laughed about it as Parker returned to his seat. But he was in absolute earnest. Earlier in the evening he had visited the suite of one of the Lions directors, only to see his backup quarterback, Tobin Rote, sitting there and enjoying a drink with Parker's bosses.

Graham was the featured speaker at the banquet and gave a tongue-in-cheek appraisal of his longtime adversaries. He said that in Cleveland there had been a standard $50 fine for any player who violated curfew. "If that held on the Detroit club," he said, "some players would go bankrupt. I won't talk any longer. The players are anxious to get the bed check over so they can start the parties."

Graham's talk was greeted with waves of laughter. Then it was Parker's turn.

"I've got a situation here I can't control anymore," he said. "These ballplayers have gotten too big for me or something. I'm getting out. There's been no life.... This is a completely dead team. I've been in football a long time...I don't want to get in the middle of another losing season."

Parker later said that there "were too many quarterbacks" on the team's board of directors. He had opposed the drafting of Heisman halfback Howard Cassady from Ohio State as the top pick of the previous year, but had been overruled by the board.

The sight of his players partying with the board, and Graham's reminders about his team's reputation, brought all these resentments boiling over. It was a situation that would be echoed eerily in just five more years in Cleveland.

Parker said later that his resignation had been "the mistake of a lifetime." But it stuck, and his longtime assistant, George Wilson, was made head coach.

Just as in 1954, the Browns and Lions met in December, right before playing for the title. Three years before it had been a "nothing" game. Both teams had clinched their divisions and Brown was slyly laying a bear trap for Detroit.

This time everything was on the line for the Lions. They had to win to stay even with the 49ers.

The Browns had never won at Briggs Stadium, and their record was kept intact in this game. The Lions contained Jim Brown and came away with a 20–7 win. But the Browns did land on Bobby Layne. The quarterback broke his ankle in a pileup on the frozen field in the Lions backfield and had to be carried off the field. The injury put him out for the rest of the season and, incidentally, changed the course of the Detroit franchise.

Detroit faced a grudge-match finale against the Bears and then a possible playoff in San Francisco before they would meet the Browns again for the title. And they would have to get it done without the man who had been their on-field and emotional leader for the last seven years.

The year before, Layne had suffered a concussion in a vicious season-closing game in Chicago. He had to come out of the game, and the Bears trounced the Lions to win the division. To make sure that would not happen again, Detroit had swung a trade with Green Bay for the veteran Rote to come in as a backup.

Now the move looked prescient. With Rote at the controls, the Lions blew past Chicago and the 49ers. They would play Cleveland for the championship for the fourth time in six years.

All the things that had gone right for Cleveland three years earlier in the 56-10 massacre blew up in their faces this time. There was no Graham to keep things on an even keel. O'Connell was still limping, and Plum was no answer.

The Lions destroyed them, 59-14. Brown broke away on a 29-yard touchdown run, but Detroit scored in every conceivable manner, including a touchdown pass by Rote off a fake field goal. It was 31-7 at the half and only got worse later on.

With that woeful experience, the two most dominant franchises in football through the 1950s settled slowly into eclipse. The Lions chose to go permanently with Rote. He had brought them through to the title, and it was feared the lingering effects of the injury could slow down Layne for good. They traded the quarterback to Pittsburgh, where his former coach, Parker, had taken over. It was not a good decision. Rote never again matched his 1957 performance, and the Lions embarked on an endless search for another Layne. They have yet to play for another title as of this writing.

As for Paul Brown, he would never get this close to the summit again.

There was stir all around the NFL. Weeb Ewbank was as good as his word in Baltimore. With the help of the two players he had snatched from under Brown's nose, Johnny Unitas and Ray Berry, among a cast of others, Ewbank took the Colts to successive championships in 1958 and 1959.

It was also a new day in New York. Cleveland's main rival would take the division title in five of the next six years, never winning a championship but always finishing ahead of the Browns. For three of those years, it was another Cleveland escapee, Y.A. Tittle, who led them. It was bad enough when he was in the other division at San Francisco. But now he was tormenting Brown directly, and the memory of how the NFL had taken Tittle away from him still rankled him.

Vince Lombardi took over at woebegone Green Bay in 1959 and in two years had the Packers playing for the championship. He would build a dynasty that won five titles in the following seven years, even bettering what Brown had done with Cleveland in the NFL. He would soon grab Brown's accustomed spot on the chart of legendary geniuses.

The ground was shifting beneath everyone's feet. The American Football League opened for business in 1960. Like its predecessor, which gave birth to the Browns, it was laughed off and ridiculed by the NFL establishment. But its wide-open, high-scoring style of play was attractive to fans who felt the older league had become too dominated by defense. The eight AFL franchises eventually thrived, competing well in New York City, and became serious rivals for the top college talent.

In that same year, the NFL voted to expand for the first time since the Browns and 49ers entered the league in 1950. The Dallas Cowboys and then the Minnesota Vikings turned out to be highly successful franchises. A former player of Brown's from his Great Lakes days, Bud Grant, would go on to coach the Vikings to the Super Bowl by the 1969 season.

Brown had enthusiastically supported Lombardi when the Green Bay management asked him about strong coaching candidates. Brown admired his performance as offensive coach of the Giants. When the Packers followed his advice and gave the job to Lombardi, Brown said he felt some responsibility for pushing so hard on his behalf. Brown drew up a short list of players who he felt could not start for Cleveland in 1959 and worked up trades with the Packers for them. In this way the Browns lost Henry Jordan, Bill Quinlan, and Willie Davis—three parts of the defensive line on which Lombardi built his dynasty.

These turned out to be terrible deals, a rank giveaway of talent. Brown defended them on the grounds that these players needed to compete regularly to reach their potential, and they would not get that opportunity in Cleveland. But there were people in the Browns organization who wondered what business it was of their coach if Lombardi did well in Green Bay. The teams did not play in the same division. That was true enough. But the Browns were no longer the all-conquering force of former years. They needed every edge they could get.

The transfer of power seemed to be formalized in 1958. Many of the Browns, in looking back on it, could pinpoint the exact moment. It came in the final game of the regular season against the Giants.

Cleveland was 9–2 and once again purring steadily along. Jim Brown was the greatest force in the league. He was averaging almost six yards per carry and scored 17 touchdowns. No one could stop him at the goal line. He gained more than 1,500 yards, and when the Browns went wide, halfback Bobby Mitchell added another 500.

Despite the coach's misgivings, Plum settled in as a regular and did an acceptable job. He started every game, threw 11 touchdown passes, and kept defenses just loose enough to open the way for the devastating Cleveland runners.

Brown had always used the short pass as the basis of his offense. Now that he had the greatest runner in football at his disposal, he adeptly switched to a rush-based offense. The old man still seemed to be right on top of it.

Cleveland was ripping through the schedule. The Browns won their first five games, scoring an average of 35 points in each contest. They hit a midseason bump, losing two in a row to the Giants and the always-troublesome Lions. But then they picked it up again to win four more.

If the Browns got a win in the finale at Yankee Stadium, they would go on to play Baltimore for the title. Even a tie would do it. New York had to win the game to force a playoff.

The Giants had dared Plum to pass against them in the earlier game. When he failed to do it, they stacked the defense against Brown and won 21–17.

In the rematch, Brown streaked 65 yards on Cleveland's first play from scrimmage. The Browns defense was able to stifle New York throughout the first half. Into the third quarter Cleveland was still holding a 10–3 lead and moving downfield.

The drive stalled at the New York 16, and the Browns lined up for another Groza field goal. He was almost automatic at this range, and the kick would give them a 13–3 lead. That would have been a huge deficit to overcome in a defense-dominated game on a snowy field.

Instead, Brown called for a fake. Holder Bobby Freeman, a former quarterback, stumbled as he got up to throw the ball, and the Giants swarmed over him.

New York then went on to tie it with a touchdown after a Jim Brown fumble, and the Giants won it in the last seconds on a 49-yard Pat Summerall field goal, 13–10. The kick made him an instant hero in New York and became Summerall's ticket to an extended network broadcasting career.

But in Cleveland the fake field goal was the play that just would not go away. Certain teams in every sport carry the memory of a certain play that seemed to shatter an entire franchise. Bill Buckner's boot in the 1986 World Series for the Red Sox. Milt Plum throwing a last-minute interception against Green Bay for the 1962 Lions. Cubs fan Steve Bartman snatching the foul fly ball away from Moises Alou in the 2003 National League playoffs. These plays haunted their teams for years, even decades. So it was with this call.

What made the play even worse was that Brown called a timeout before sending in the play, almost tipping off the Giants that something was up. Some of the Cleveland players said later they heard the New York defense yelling, "It's a fake," even before the ball was snapped.

It was simply inexplicable. Even the Cleveland writers, who rarely wrote a discouraging word about their resident genius, couldn't understand it. There were even rumors, according to writer Terry Pluto in his book *When All the World Was Browns Town*, that the team had tanked it to set up another big payday in a playoff game. It was an outrageous assertion and ridiculous to anyone who knew Brown. But the play hung over his head and wouldn't go away.

Brown always argued that his logic was sound. Another touchdown would have made it 17–3. Because the Giants had to win to force a playoff game, they would have been forced to score three times.

There was also a terrible blown call by the officials late in the game. With the score tied, 10–10, Frank Gifford appeared to fumble a pass. The Browns' Walt Michaels picked it up and started to run for the clinching touchdown. The New York players were throwing their helmets to the turf in disgust, believing the game was all but over.

Instead, the officials ruled it was an incomplete pass. The films showed that Gifford had taken as many as six steps before losing the ball. But the call stood. No instant replay, no appeal. The Giants were alive, Pat Summerall kicked his famous field goal, and the same two teams would meet again at Yankee Stadium the following week.

In later years, Brown would muse that if only the call on Gifford's fumble had been right how different the future of the Browns would have been. He never talked much about the fake field goal.

Cleveland had nothing left for the playoff game. Brown said later that the team had "lost faith in Plum's ability to play under stress." The quarterback did throw a critical interception to Huff in the 10-0 loss.

But it was an unfair slap at Plum. Virtually to a man, the Browns were convinced they had been placed in that position only because the old man had blown it the week before.

It wasn't Plum the team had lost faith in.

Brown had always favored the autocratic style. Although he encouraged his players to call him by his first name ("This is a friendly place"), there was mounting evidence that the Browns were not happy with this benevolent despotism.

Something Frank Gatski said after leaving the team was an indicator. He was one of the original Browns, a starting center and future Hall of Fame player. He was traded to the Lions before the 1957 season and became a major element in their championship run. But it was what he said halfway through the year that was telling: "I had no idea that football could be so much fun."

Fun was not part of the game plan with Brown, and as his team slipped back into the unfamiliar swamps of mediocrity, fun became increasingly scarce.

His players were afraid of him; afraid of the withering stare and the biting remarks on movie days. They were afraid of being personally singled out for losing a game, a practice that was becoming more common. Even Groza, one of Brown's personal favorites, was told after a missed kick, "You're killing our football team."

Renfro, who had performed so well on past championship teams, was informed on the sidelines, "You can't make the big catch anymore." Brown said he regretted the words, but they had been said. Those who heard them never forgot how stricken Renfro was.

And these were his favorites, veterans of the good years. Newcomers never knew what to expect.

When rookie linebacker Mike Lucci showed up at his first training camp in 1962, Brown walked up to him and snapped, "I see you're from Tennessee. Well, unless you work out better than the last player we took from Tennessee, you won't be here long."

Lucci walked away muttering, "What the hell?"

He asked a veteran what was going on. "I was told the last guy from Tennessee had been Doug Atkins. Brown traded him to the Bears because Doug was not someone who abided by all the rules. Atkins turned into an All-Pro. Brown was still mad about it and took it out on me."

Every man who joined the Browns was aware that he was playing for a legend, a larger-than-life figure. Brown understood the source of his power and could cut the players down to size with a word.

Even back in Massillon very few players said that they loved the coach. But now there were those who hated him. By the same token, a few words of praise and these same men were walking on air. But the praise was harder to come by. The big chill had descended on the Browns.

The team also was convinced the coach's thinking had chilled, frozen in the past, too conservative. The game had left him behind.

Brown was a part owner of the franchise, and the players thought that was reflected in the penurious contracts they received. One of the big reasons he gave his preseason talk about keeping wives separate from football was his certain knowledge that when the men got together with their wives, the talk, inevitably, would turn to salaries. He didn't want any of that.

The Browns were 7-5 in 1959, and 8-3-1 the following year. They finished second in the division both times.

Jim Brown continued to come through, rushing for 2,586 yards in these two seasons. Mitchell wasn't far behind with 1,249 yards. There was still talent on both sides of the line. The Browns had continued to draft well. Gene Hickerson and Dick Schafrath joined McCormack on the offensive line. Paul Wiggin, Bob Gain, Walt Michaels, Galen Fiss, and Bernie Parrish were all standouts on defense.

But whatever Plum did at quarterback, it wasn't enough for Brown. Over these same two years, Plum threw for 35 touchdowns and only 13 interceptions. In 1960, using the rating system then in vogue, which was weighted heavily toward passing efficiency, he came in at a spectacular 110.4. When you could throw screen passes to Jim Brown, the numbers piled up.

Still, Plum wasn't Graham. Never would be. Brown was convinced that they wouldn't win with him because he folded in the big games.

In 1959, with the team running right behind the Giants late in the season, the Browns lost three in a row. Two of them were by a single point, and the third was a 48-7 blowout in New York. The two close games were the kind Graham used to find a way to win. Those were games won by Brown's "November teams." Plum hadn't done a November kind of job.

In 1960, with the Browns superior to the eventual champion Philadelphia Eagles in every statistical category, they again lost two critical midseason games. An offense that averaged 30 points per game could get no more than 13 against two also-rans. It had to be Plum.

Plum, in turn, chafed under Brown's rules. He felt they gave him no room to maneuver. Brown toyed with the idea of playing his backup, Jim Ninowski, but ended up trading him to Detroit. Even the once-coveted Len Dawson came to Cleveland, but Brown didn't feel he was the answer either.

So he stuck with Plum and fumed. It just wasn't coming together.

To some of the Browns it was also starting to look as though their star was permitted to run outside the rules. The Plum-Ninowski quarterback controversy was a major issue in Cleveland. Jim Brown had a regular commentary on the radio that was written by popular sports columnist Hal Lebovitz. The coach didn't like this at all, and when the player used the segment to campaign for Plum, the coach hit the roof.

"No sooner was the show over, my phone rang," Lebovitz would write in 2001. "Paul Brown. He knew I was writing the show. 'Hal, how could you let this guy say those things? You know better than that,' and so forth.

"And I said, 'Paul, this is his show. I just write the words. Here's his phone number. Call Jim.'"

Lebovitz phoned Jim Brown to give him a heads-up that his coach was angry and intended to call him.

"No, he won't," said Brown. And he never did. But the coach barely spoke to Lebovitz for years afterward.

The players saw what was happening. While they admired the running back's gifts and what he brought to the team, they knew a different set of rules applied to him. That wasn't the sort of system their coach preached. But it was the system now in effect for his team. Even when Jim Brown messed up a play, the coach would criticize someone else who may have been blameless. And his blocking wasn't getting any better either.

Late in the 1960 season, the Browns blasted the Bears 42–0 in the final home game. Only 38,000 fans turned out. Among them was a young advertising executive from New York who watched with special interest and began dreaming of ways to fill all those seats.

His name was Art Modell, and he had just been offered a chance to buy the Cleveland Browns.

The architect of Paul Brown's departure from the team he had created was then 35 years old. Modell understood what the NFL was becoming. He had come out of the culture of television and knew how to market, how to sell, how to create celebrities.

All of that was anathema to Brown. Their collision was as fast as it was inevitable.

Modell grew up in Brooklyn. His father had lost his business during the Depression, had to go on the road as a salesman, and died alone in a Texas hotel room when Modell was only 14.

No one had handed him anything. He wasn't some rich kid who wanted to own a football team as a toy. He was an aggressive businessman who saw an opportunity. But in the rough parlance of sports, he was also a jock sniffer. He loved hanging around athletes, idolized some of them. The thought of having dinner with Jim Brown blew him away. To actually own the Cleveland Browns, still carrying the reputation as the greatest team in football...well, he wasn't going to let this chance pass him by.

The syndicate headed by David Jones named its price as $4 million. Modell jumped at it. Most football observers thought he'd been robbed. The Jones group had paid just $600,000 for the franchise in 1953. But Modell gathered up some partners, and on January 25, 1961, he closed the deal.

Brown had been a 15 percent owner of the Browns, and Modell paid him off with a check for $500,000. Brown would now be an employee. A very well paid employee, to be sure. Brown had been working with an eight-year contract calling for $50,000 annually. Modell tore that deal up and made it for $82,500. No coach anywhere was making that kind of money in 1961. The new owner regarded Brown as one of the assets he had just purchased. He was awed by him as much as any of the players.

Brown assumed the old arrangement that had been in effect during the McBride and Jones years would remain, that he would be given a free hand in handling matters "essential to the football operation." There he was quite mistaken. Modell had declared that he wanted to be a "playing owner." Brown didn't know what that meant, but he didn't like the sound of it. Modell also moved his residence from New York to Cleveland so he could be closer to the team he owned.

When Modell was interviewed by *The Plain Dealer*, he set out to reassure everyone.

"In my opinion, [Paul Brown] has no peer as a football coach. His record speaks for itself. I view our relationship as a working partnership.... We will be consulting frequently. We'll be partners in the Browns operation."

The coach read the interview and was not amused. He saw, instead, the dark clouds rolling in. Partnership? Consulting? What was that? Didn't this kid understand the way things always were done on the Browns?

Modell said that in their first meeting, after the season-ending 1960 game with the Giants in New York, he called Brown "a living legend" right to his face. That would change in a hurry because Paul Brown may have been an asset, but Jim Brown was a megastar.

Modell was convinced that the Browns hadn't done nearly enough to build up their star running back on a national basis, to turn him into the biggest attraction in football. That's how you sell 80,000 tickets a game.

Modell would become one of the most influential owners in the NFL because he understood how the greater game was played. He knew the economics of television intimately and would show the other owners how to shake the money tree. Within a year Modell led negotiations that resulted in a $4.65 million contract with CBS, the biggest television contract the NFL had signed. He was the leading advocate for *Monday Night Football*. By 1998 the television deal with all networks that he had first put in motion would be worth $17.6 billion over eight years. Modell was the wave of the future. Before long, he decided that his coach, the "living legend," had mired his football team in the past.

If a team owner hangs out with his employees for any length of time, he will hear complaints. Lots of complaints. Professional athletes are notorious crybabies. Some franchises have a history of favored athletes running to the owner whenever they didn't like what the coach or manager was doing. In many cases, the coach or manager was soon history. Modell was single, had lots of money to spend, and was only a few years older than most of the players. They talked to him, and what he heard amazed him.

Far from revering the coach, many of the players couldn't stand him. They didn't like his offensive scheme, his cutting remarks, his endless rules. Among the most persistent of complainers was Jim Brown.

Paul Brown was aware of what was happening. Still, he was confident that he knew how to handle his superstar. More than that, he was building a winning team again. It was taking longer than he liked, but he was sure the pieces were slowly coming together.

He didn't know it, but the clock was already ticking down on him. If he was aware of that on some level, he never consciously believed it. Paul Brown was the Cleveland Browns. He couldn't be judged by the same measure as other coaches. This was his team, and he would make it rise again.

Groza returned to the Browns in 1961 after announcing his retirement and sitting out the entire previous season. The circumstances around that decision illustrate the deteriorating relationship between Brown and Modell.

Groza's back problems were so severe that he could no longer play on the offensive line. Brown did not want to take up a roster spot with a man who was only a place kicker. So he brought in Sam Baker to do all the kicking, field goals, and punts, and Groza went off to sell life insurance.

But to Modell, Groza as a kicker was plenty good enough because he was also an attraction. He was "the Toe." When Groza came on the field to attempt a late, game-deciding field goal, the Cleveland crowds went bonkers. This was what Modell wanted—excitement, pizzazz, and to hell with the roster.

The new owner took the initiative and got in touch with Groza on his own. Modell found that Groza was only too eager to return to the Browns.

Modell approached Brown with the idea and found the coach highly skeptical. Then a few days later he saw statements in the newspaper that made it appear as if Groza's return was all the coach's idea. Modell didn't like that.

For Brown's part, he'd been given reports of Modell sitting in the press box and audibly second-guessing decisions made on the field. He went to the owner and told him that such behavior would undercut the coach's authority and, worse yet, make the team look ridiculous.

"I'm just a fan," Modell responded, according to Brown.

"No, you're not," said Brown. "You're the owner."

Modell also believed in hyping expectations, describing several of his players as the best in the league at their position. To Modell it was just part of the old showbiz routine. But to Brown it opened the door to all sorts of speculation. If the individual Browns were so good, why weren't they winning more? Could it be the coach?

It turned out that 1961 was another desultory season. Cleveland went 8–5–1 and was trampled at home by the Giants, 37–21, before a full house in a game that knocked the Browns out of the race.

Plum continued to chafe under the play-calling restrictions. He argued that defenses would shift late in the count against the Browns, and he felt locked into the play called by the coach. Modell agreed with him. But when Plum made the mistake of questioning the system in public, he was gone. Traded to Detroit for Ninowski, whom the coach had always preferred. Modell went along with the deal. He knew that Plum lacked star quality as a quarterback. He was ready for a different look.

It was the other big off-season deal, however, that led to the ultimate rupture in the relationship between the owner and his coach.

As good as the Jim Brown-Mitchell tandem was, the coach felt it would be even better if his star back had a more effective blocker. The two men had run for 1,956 yards in 1961. But the coach felt that Jim Brown had no ceiling on his talent, and the running back needed another big back to clear the way for him. Coach Brown knew just where to find the back he needed. It was right where he found Brown: at Syracuse University. He wanted Ernie Davis.

Davis had broken all of Brown's rushing and scoring records with the Orangemen. It was Brown, in fact, who was sent in to recruit him for Syracuse. In his sophomore year, 1959, he led them to an undefeated season and their only national championship. As a senior, he won the Heisman Trophy. Everyone who knew Davis raved about his character. If Brown had set out to mold the perfect player, it might have been this kid.

The coach's relationship with Jim Brown was now on the edgy side. The coach overlooked a lot that would have brought down the thunder on lesser talents—such as Plum. He also knew that the fullback and the owner had become close off the field. Buddies. On one occasion Brown had to delay his practice while a conversation between Modell and the player wound down. The practice timetable was inviolable to Paul Brown—this is where games were won—but he bit his tongue.

Davis, however, seemed more like Paul Brown's kind of guy. The only trouble was Washington had the draft rights. So the deal was cut— Bobby Mitchell for Ernie Davis. In Brown's mind, it was a perfect exchange.

But when Modell got a phone call from Redskins owner George Preston Marshall asking him how he liked the deal, the Browns owner hit the roof. He had been cut out of the talks completely. Brown had run this one on his own.

The two men were communicating from different planets. Modell knew that he was the team's owner. Brown didn't care. He ran the football organization. That's the way it always was, and that's how his contact said it would be. At least, that's what Brown thought it said.

The Davis trade was going over big in Cleveland, however, so Modell got over his petulance. Instead, he took on the task of signing him. The AFL was still competing for college players, and the Buffalo Bills had the rights to Davis. So everyone knew the bidding would go high. It went very high, to $80,000 a year with a no-cut contract.

Now it was Brown's turn to go ballistic. Yes, he had wanted Davis. But he had never in his life given anyone a no-cut deal. In Brown's mind such security destroyed incentive and made it impossible for him to coach the player. On top of that, it was $30,000 more a year than Cleveland was paying Jim Brown. Modell may have thought of his star player as a great buddy. He even referred to him as "my senior partner," another locution that sent the coach into a tizzy. But Paul Brown knew that when Jim read that story, there was going to be big trouble.

There was one positive development during the off-season, though. In a deal that did not attract much attention, the Browns got a backup for Ninowski. Frank Ryan had filled a similar role with the Rams. After demanding a trade, he was not happy to learn that he was going to Cleveland. He figured that only meant more bench time because Ninowski had an in he couldn't match. The Browns had just traded for him as a starter, and it was known that Paul Brown liked the starter.

But Ryan had other attributes. For one thing, he tested off the charts. No one had ever passed these tests Brown so admired with Ryan's scores. He had been a physics major at Rice, which was not exactly a football factory. As a professional player, he was working on a doctorate in math during the off-season. Sportswriters of the time had him talking in algebra and diagramming quadratic equations in the clubhouse. But while Ryan was a brilliant man, he also was a football guy.

The more he saw of him, the more Brown suspected he had finally found his new Otto Graham. A player who could match his physical skills with mental skills.

"He's no schoolboy," said the coach. "If he continues to improve this deal could exceed all the others."

When Ninowski went down with a shoulder injury, Ryan stepped in. At the end of the season, he had better stats than the nominal starter in almost every category. Brown was more convinced than ever that this was the man he'd been waiting for.

But the season also became a tragic disappointment to the Browns. The team had found a quarterback but lost its next star before he ever had a chance to shine.

The troubles began at the College All-Star Game. Davis had to get some teeth pulled, and his recovery from the minor surgery was puzzlingly slow and painful. The doctors ran some tests and made a terrible discovery: he had leukemia. Their prognosis was that Davis had no more than a few months to live.

The organization was stunned by the news. Davis returned to Cleveland and began a regimen of chemotherapy to control the disease. By October the cancer had gone into remission, and Davis said he wanted to play.

Brown consulted friends at the Cleveland Clinic and was told that under no circumstances should that be allowed to happen. With heavy physical contact, a reversal could occur.

The Browns were struggling on the field, losing two of their first three games. With neither Davis nor Mitchell in the lineup, Jim Brown, who also was hampered by a wrist injury, was off to the worst start of his career. He would finish at fewer than 1,000 yards rushing—albeit only by four yards—for only the second time in his career. Charley Scales and Tom Wilson, the two new halfbacks in the Browns' scheme, could not pick up the slack. It was becoming clear that the 1962 season was headed down the tubes.

Here is where the stories begin to diverge.

According to Brown, everyone on the team knew that Davis would never play again. Modell, however, kept holding out that hope. He told reporters that Davis was working out under medical supervision and could be cleared to get into a game.

Finally, Brown said in his autobiography, "Modell came to me one day and said, 'Put him in a game, and let him play. We have a big investment in him, and I'd like a chance to get some of it back. It doesn't matter how long he plays; just let him run back a kick, let him do anything, just so we can get a story in the paper saying he's going to play, and the fans will come to see him. If he has to go, why not let him have a little fun?'"

Brown added that he was told by NFL Commissioner Pete Rozelle, who was close with Modell, that the league would overrule any attempt to put Davis in a game.

Modell heatedly denied any such conversation took place. Davis had come to him pleading for a chance to play, he said, and he simply wanted to grant the wish of a dying man. There were also physicians, according to sportswriter Lebovitz, who told Modell that playing would do Davis no harm.

They reached a compromise: Davis would wear a Browns uniform, be introduced before a game, and run across the field in a spotlight. He received a standing ovation, the only time he ever appeared at Cleveland Stadium.

Davis died seven months later.

The Brown-Modell relationship went from chilly to frozen after this episode. Modell had guaranteed a title for the Browns during the preseason. Instead, the team was staggering to its worst showing since the losing season of 1956.

The emergence of Ryan as a potential starter was encouraging. But under pressure from Modell, several players (including Jim Brown), and the media, Brown was forced to back down from his cherished system of sending in every play with messenger guards. Again, he reached a compromise, agreeing to use the messengers only in certain situations. But he was simply buying time, hoping that everyone would come to their senses and realize his way was best.

Still, abandoning this part of his system, if only temporarily, heightened Brown's sense that control was slipping rapidly from his grasp.

Then there was Blanton Collier. He had been unsuccessful in his eight-year effort to turn around the University of Kentucky football program. He did wind up with a winning record, a rarity for any football coach in that basketball-mad school. But he was fired at the end of the 1961 season.

He asked Brown for a job, and although there really wasn't an opening, Brown created the post of offensive backfield coach to take on his old friend. Collier was more than a friend, really. He was almost family. There was never any question about Brown's sense of loyalty.

But soon he began questioning Collier's. He heard reports that Collier had been invited on golf outings with Modell. To Brown's mind this sounded suspiciously like another attempt to isolate him. The owner already had accomplished that with several of his players. Now it appeared he was after Brown's assistant coaches.

Collier had been responsible for modifications in the messenger guard system, designing a series of check-off options for the quarterback. As Brown grew more wary of his relationship with Modell, he took away that job. The end result was that Collier, with too little to occupy his time, drew even closer to the owner.

Defensive players were also going to Modell, complaining that all the changes the coach had made were designed to strengthen the offensive unit. They felt the Browns were unable to compete in a league that was increasingly dominated by defensive teams.

Brown felt besieged, surrounded by ingrates, misunderstood. As the season collapsed around him, he withdrew. The season ended with a road win in San Francisco. But it was not a happy trip. During a flight delay, Modell sat in the airport bar buying drinks for players. This broke a hard-and-fast Brown rule. He had thrown players off the team for drinking in public during the season. Now the owner was standing the drinks for them.

According to some players, Modell also was asking pointed questions about Brown and Collier.

Some descriptions of what was happening called it a "players' revolt." Jim Brown was named as the head mutineer. There is no doubt that the coach's relationship with his star tracked fairly much the same as the coach's relationship with the owner. Paul Brown felt the tight buddy-buddy act between Jim Brown and Modell was unhealthy for everyone and was making it impossible for him to maintain discipline.

The coach even seethed inside about Brown's practice of walking back to the huddle after a tackle instead of trotting.

"They only pay me to run forward. They don't pay me to go to the huddle," the running back told McCormack.

The offensive lineman, long a Paul Brown stalwart, sympathized with the running back. After all, he was carrying the ball approximately 30 times a game. So what if his blocking left a bit to be desired? Look at everything else he brought to the table.

And this was the attitude of a player who always had considered himself a Paul Brown loyalist. But McCormack was increasingly disgusted at the turmoil tearing at the Browns. The attitudes of other veterans were about the same or worse. Something had to give.

Jim Brown always denied going to Modell and stating that either the coach had to go or he would. There was no denying, however, that the star player had spoken out on several occasions about how sick he was of constantly being made to run between the tackles. He also complained later that in all his years with the Browns he had never been invited to the coach's home. But the fact is, none of the players were. That wasn't how the coach related to his players. Modell made them his buddies, but Brown never would.

The prime mover among the dissidents actually seemed to be defensive back Parrish. But while Jim Brown did not actually wield the hatchet, there is no doubt he approved of its use.

Coach Brown had already started looking forward to the 1963 season. It would be his 18th at the helm of the Browns, and despite the poor record of the previous season he saw better days ahead. The rebuilding plan was working. He was sure of it.

But he was already gone. Modell had met with Rozelle secretly and told him he intended to fire Brown. It was such an extraordinary decision that even Modell, for all his brashness, felt he had to let the commissioner know.

Rozelle was staggered. He was aware of the estrangement between the two men. But this was Paul Brown they were talking about. Paul Brown! How do you fire the guy for whom the team is named?

But Modell felt there was no turning back.

On January 7, 1963, an ordinary Monday, he called Brown into his office and dropped the bomb.

Again the two men presented very different versions of what happened.

According to Brown, Modell told him: "I've made a decision. You have to step down as coach and general manager.... This team can never be fully mine as long as you are here because whenever anyone thinks of the Browns they think of you. Every time I come to the stadium I feel that I am invading your domain, and from now on there can only be one dominant image."

Modell's version of this meeting is much shorter. No sooner had he told Brown of his decision, he said, and informed him that he would be "reassigned," than the coach stormed out of his office without saying another word.

They didn't agree on what happened next either. In Brown's version he looked outside the front door of his house the next morning, and there were the contents of his office sitting in cardboard boxes on his porch.

Modell insisted, however, that Brown came back to his office to clean it out and saw his entire staff of assistants, including Collier, hard at work watching game films. This so dismayed him that he left without taking his stuff. Modell said he had no choice but to have it delivered to Brown's home.

Modell wavered in later years over whether any of this was the right thing to do. He told different stories on different occasions. But in several interviews Modell said that maybe he should have tried to work things out.

Because, after all, this was Paul Brown.

14

1970: Cincinnati Bengals 30, Cleveland Browns 27

There was an extended newspaper strike in Cleveland when Paul Brown got the ax. Many observers felt that's why Art Modell timed the firing as he did. He was always a master of public relations. When the news got out, though, it still came as a shock. It had been eight years since the Browns last ruled football. But Coach Brown occupied a place in the city that seemed as secure as the statue of its founder, Moses Cleaveland, down in Public Square.

This wasn't about firing a coach. This was about ending an era.

"I couldn't assimilate it," says Arnold Blostein, now an attorney in Fort Lauderdale, Florida, but a native Clevelander. "I was just out of high school that winter, and I'd grown up with the Browns. Motley, Graham—they were my childhood heroes. And the Browns were Paul Brown. It was just unimaginable that they could be coached by anyone else."

At Johnny's Bar, a hangout for Browns fans on the city's near west side, "we were all stunned," says Eugene Santosuosso, whose family owns the restaurant. "He was football, and from all I knew of him quite a nice person. Browns fans didn't like it too well.

"But, you know, it passed, and good things started to happen, and Browns fans stick with their team. As far as I was concerned, Modell was a regular customer at our place. I guess, bottom line, business is business."

Although the boom was lowered on a Monday, the Browns didn't announce the change until 5:15 PM on Wednesday, and then only through a terse press release. Modell did not appear to answer questions, although he did respond to phone calls.

"They tried to make it appear as if this was a friendly little shift to give employment to the man who paints names on the office doors," wrote Seymour Rothman, of the *Toledo Blade*. He said that Modell gave no specific reason for the move, except to repeat, "We did what we believe to be in the best interests of the Browns."

When asked if the team would change its name now that Brown was no longer running it, Modell emphatically dismissed such a possibility. "This is the image we've created," he said. "We're still the Browns."

Modell loved the brand. He just didn't care for the product.

The Associated Press called the news "startling" but mostly because of the absence of "the usual pretense that this was a mutual decision."

The predominant emotion was, indeed, more astonishment than resentment. Browns fans had heard about the complaints by the players. They had read about the interior squabbling. They could read the scoreboard. They just never believed Modell would actually do it.

Neither could Brown. His new title was vice president, but his duties were not made clear. In fact, he had almost none. Brown would describe it to reporters as "vice president in charge of I don't know what."

"I was told long ago that if you stay in coaching long enough everything will happen to you," he said. "Well, it has happened to me—and I never thought it would."

For the most part, though, Brown kept silent and let the bitterness rage inside. His attorneys looked at his contract and assured him there was nothing else he could do. Modell was within his legal rights. They advised him to just sit back and cash the $82,500 in yearly paychecks.

After a few days he started making phone calls in the mistaken belief that his staff of assistant coaches would be job hunting. Don Shula, his former player, had just been named head coach of the Colts and assured Brown that he would find a place there for Collier.

He needn't have bothered. Collier already had been told the Browns head coaching job was his, and the staff of assistants would be retained. Modell wasn't altogether comfortable with the decision. Collier was rather reticent, not the media-friendly, charismatic leader that he wanted. But Modell was still a novice in the NFL. He was smart enough to know that Collier was an experienced, highly competent coach.

To Brown, this was the cruelest cut of all. His closest associate saw the blow fall and then went about his business as if nothing were amiss.

For the next five years, Brown would be a shadow. Cut off from the game he loved. Estranged from people he thought were his friends. An irrelevance in the city he had come to think of as home.

And the cream of the jest was that the Browns began to win big. He'd been right about all the personnel moves he made. Ryan was rapidly growing into one of the top quarterbacks in the league. Ernie Green became the second big back that Brown wanted to block for Jim Brown. Lombardi was overstocked at the position and had sent Green over to the Browns as a sort of reciprocal gift for the players Brown had sent him. Gary Collins, the top pick in the 1962 draft, became a reliable, big-play receiver. Almost all the starters were returnees from his last team.

The new-old Browns won their first six games of the 1963 season before finally settling back to a 10-4 record. It was yet another second-place finish to the Giants. But Brown finished with 1,863 yards rushing. He and Collins combined for 28 of the 42 touchdowns the offensive team would score. Best of all from Modell's standpoint, the crowds started to build. Four times in the seven home games more than 75,000 fans were in the stadium, and two of the games were sellouts.

Then the Browns won it all. The final piece of the puzzle arrived in the form of Paul Warfield. At Ohio State, where the pass was regarded as a form of pestilence by Woody Hayes, Warfield had been used as a running back. Sometimes Hayes used him as a defensive back, where his sprinter's speed enabled him to cover any receiver in the Big Ten. But there was no question that his best position would be as a wideout.

One of the functions that Brown did carry out in his new role was as a scout of college talent. Warfield had the attributes he always had sought in his players: character, speed, and an Ohio pedigree. Brown wrote a short note to Modell urging Cleveland to make Warfield its top pick in the 1964 draft.

Brown saw him as a defensive back because that seemed to be the team's most urgent need. He also detested Parrish, a holdover at cornerback, because Brown learned that he had been one of his most vocal detractors to Modell. If Brown's advice had been followed, Warfield may well have taken his job. Instead, Collier turned Warfield into a receiver, and he burned up the league, averaging 18 yards on his 52 catches and scoring nine touchdowns.

With two outstanding wide receivers and the strengthened backfield combination, the Browns were almost unstoppable. They went 10-3-1 and punctuated the season by destroying the hated Giants, 52-20, in the season's final game at Yankee Stadium.

Then they went on and upset Shula's favored Colts, 27-0, in the championship game at Cleveland Stadium. Ryan threw three touchdown passes to Collins, and the Browns defense stifled the great Unitas almost completely.

After nine long years the Browns had brought it all back home while averaging 78,000 fans per game. Modell was exultant. It had worked out perfectly, just as he had planned.

Modell had only one dissatisfaction: he never got a congratulatory message from Brown.

The coach traveled and spent more time with his beloved wife, Katy. They decided to move from a city that had suddenly turned cold to La Jolla, California, the idyllic seaside area near San Diego.

In 1967, after the mandatory five-year waiting period, he was inducted into the Pro Football Hall of Fame. His inclusion was as automatic as a Groza field goal. Brown never needed to accomplish another thing. His place in football history was absolutely secure.

Yet Brown was miserable.

"I had everything a man could want," he said. "Leisure, enough money, a wonderful family. Yet with all of that I was eating my heart out. Football had been my life. I had a strong desire to become alive again."

So he explored other coaching possibilities, all of which fell short of his expectations. He'd had his fill of intrusive, troublesome owners. At the first indication of any problem like that at the interview Brown was out the door.

He was looking for control. He understood now that in order for his system to work he had to be the man in charge. No more Modells crashing the party.

As for Modell, the big party had ended in Cleveland. The 1964 championship was to be the only one the Browns ever won under Modell's ownership. The team went back to the title game in 1965 and lost to Green Bay. After that, his "senior partner" and buddy, Jim Brown, went Hollywood.

While Brown was filming *The Dirty Dozen* in England, the shooting schedule ran long. Brown told Modell that he would be late for the 1966 preseason training camp. The owner did not take it well. He threatened to fine Brown for every day he missed. This was a challenge to Modell's authority, and he had shown Paul Brown what happened to people who did that.

Jim Brown was 30 years old, still in his prime. Had he remained in football he surely could have finished with a career rushing record so high it would never be broken. But he was also a proud man at a time when black athletes were beginning to assert themselves as players in the national civil rights drama. Brown would not be threatened. He quit and never came back.

In later years, just as he had with Paul Brown, Modell wondered if he could have been more conciliatory and given his star a little room. But Jim Brown had left the house, and the team Paul Brown had crafted began a steady decline.

As the NFL continued to wax fat, it added more teams. Atlanta and New Orleans joined the league in the mid-1960s, and the rival AFL placed a team in Miami. That move brought the AFL's membership to nine. The odd number made for some awkward scheduling, and the league was eager to add a tenth franchise. The likeliest candidate was Cincinnati.

The demographics were good, there was a civic willingness to get behind a franchise and build a stadium, and a local ownership group had emerged. There was also tremendous momentum in Ohio to get Brown back into the coaching business with another team in the state. Even the governor got involved, lobbying hard for the Cincinnati franchise and pulling in political favors.

One potential obstacle was Modell, who could have argued that the new team would intrude on his territorial rights. But he did not and, in fact, gave his support to it.

The franchise fee was $9 million, and Brown became the team's third-largest investor, with the title of coach and general manager. More important, he was named the voting trustee of the franchise, meaning that he was its sole representative in all league matters. These were owners like he once had in Cleveland, perfectly content to let him run the show.

Brown was not terribly enthusiastic about the team being in the AFL. But he soon learned that behind the scenes a merger between the two leagues was already cooking. By the summer of 1967 it was a done deal, with the final realignment scheduled for the 1970 season.

As part of the agreement, three teams from the NFL would join the former AFL franchises to create the American Football Conference. The three that made the shift were the Baltimore Colts, Pittsburgh Steelers...and the Cleveland Browns.

Both the Browns and the Bengals were placed in the conference's Central Division. That meant they would play each other twice a year, starting in 1970.

But that was still three years away. In the meantime, Brown had a team to build.

The years, the frustrations were washed away. Suddenly it was 1946 again. He was starting with a clean slate, putting together a new team. His kind of team. He wouldn't have the sort of free access he had to talent back then, but it was a noble endeavor, just the same.

The Cincinnati Reds had agreed to pitch in and help build a new multipurpose stadium on the Ohio River. But Riverfront Stadium would not be ready until 1970. Until then, the team would play at the University of Cincinnati's home field, Nippert Stadium. It held fewer than 30,000, a far cry from the massive Lakefront facility in Cleveland. But that didn't bother Brown.

He knew the territory. He'd gone to college at Miami University, just a few miles outside Cincinnati. It was a different part of the state, culturally and economically, from Cleveland. But it was still Ohio, and Paul Brown knew Ohio.

The first order of business was picking a name. There would be no vote of the fans this time. Brown chose it himself. The Bengals. There had been a pro team in Cincinnati with that name in the late 1930s, part of the old American Football League. Brown thought it "would provide a link with (the) past."

Oddly enough, he had rejected the name Panthers in Cleveland because it had been associated with a previous professional team in that city. He had said that he wanted nothing that "smacked of failure." But that was then.

The bengal is also a tiger; just like the mascot of Massillon Washington High School. Its colors are orange and black. Brown thought those hues would look quite nice on his new team's uniforms. And if they closely resembled the color pattern of the Browns...well, what of it?

For once he would be relaxed going into the new season. He knew that high expectations were unrealistic with a first-year expansion team. It wasn't like Cleveland, where every season held a potential championship.

His son, Mike, had moved into the executive offices of the new team as his father's top assistant and most trusted aide. He had obtained the law degree that his father had once intended to pursue, and he got it from Harvard, too.

Mike had watched his father's humiliation in Cleveland and swore that the Brown family would never again go through anything like that.

"He was a demanding boss," says Mike Brown, who is now president and owner of the Bengals. "He expected everyone to perform at their best level in whatever capacity they were in. That included me. He had a way of getting me to respond fast and without much debate, if any.

"My father had a very lively sense of humor—quick-witted, fun to be around. He was a different person on the golf course. He had a defective drive, fell away from the ball. But from 150 yards in, he could have gone on the tour.

"When he was tending to business he was serious. I think people misunderstood some of the things he said about his players. He used words he never would have used otherwise, but that's the way players talk. They may not always have loved him, but they loved the results."

In addition to positioning his son as his top aide, there was the matter of picking a staff of assistants. Bill Johnson, who would succeed Brown as head coach of the Bengals, was hired from the 49ers. Rick Forzano, who would go on to coach the Lions, came aboard as backfield coach. The receivers coach would be Bill Walsh, who had been coaching a semipro team in California. He immersed himself in Brown's offensive theories, and a decade later, they would reemerge as Walsh's West Coast offense with San Francisco.

Separate from the coaches, among Brown's first hires was George Bird, his entertainment director from Massillon and Cleveland. He still intended to give the folks a good show, even if the football might fall short of his standards.

The AFL teams were not about to do the new team any favors in the expansion draft. The Bengals came in with more restrictive terms than had been given Miami a few years prior. Moreover, the Dolphins were exempt from losing any of their players.

In Brown's mind, the league was doing him a favor. He did not want retreads. Instead, he would build from the college draft. That had always been an important part of his system. He prided himself on going into the draft meeting better prepared than anyone else, with the most highly organized scouting reports in the league. Other teams had caught up with his methods. He even suspected some of them at peeking at his lists. But he was ready for this draft.

Bob Johnson, the first pick, would become Cincinnati's starting center for the next decade. Paul Robinson had slipped under the radar because he only started as a senior at Arizona. The Bengals grabbed him, and he led the league in rushing in 1968.

The first draft furnished four starters on defense, two on the offensive line, and tight end Bob Trumpy, who would go on to an outstanding career with the Bengals.

The Bengals then astonished everyone by winning two of their first three games of that 1968 season. But it was an illusion. They went on to perform as expected, losing 10 of their last 11 games to finish 3-11.

They desperately needed a quarterback. Brown didn't have to look too far to find one. He'd been playing right on the same field as the Bengals. Greg Cook had starred with Cincinnati, setting an NCAA passing record in one game. He was big and had a strong arm. Best of all, he came from Dayton. He was another of Brown's prized Ohio boys.

The Bengals named him their top choice in the 1969 draft, and he immediately stepped in as their starter. He led the AFL in passing, averaging better than 17 yards per completion. The team defeated that season's Super Bowl winners, Kansas City, and Cook was named the league's Offensive Rookie of the Year.

That honor was complemented by linebacker Bill Bergey being named the Defensive Rookie of the Year. And the Coach of the Year was Paul Brown.

The Bengals had actually run up a winning record at home, winning the first three games on their schedule in 1969, all of them at Nippert Stadium. But they could produce only a tie in their seven road games and finished at 4-9-1.

Still, it was an improvement, and the Bengals seemed to be on their way to great things.

Before the 1969 season started, however, the coach's beloved Katy died of a heart attack while undergoing surgery. She had been his sweetheart, best friend, support, and rock for more than four decades. And just as he was embarking on this great new venture, she was gone.

He buried her in Massillon, Ohio, where they had met and which they always thought of as home.

The 1970 season began with huge expectations. Riverfront Stadium was ready, with a seating capacity of almost 60,000. Most games at Nippert had been near sellouts, but that meant an average of approximately 27,000 tickets each game. The move to the bigger stadium would quickly improve the Bengals' profitability.

The emergence of Cook, the steady improvements on defense, outstanding receivers, and the transformation of Jess Phillips from defensive back to ball carrier, all seemed to betoken great things. And then there was Brown, anointed once more as the best coach in the game. Cincinnati could hardly wait for this season to begin.

The Bengals were now fully integrated into the NFL and would start play in the AFC Central Division. The week of November 15 had been circled long in advance. It would be the first visit of the Cleveland Browns to Cincinnati. The two teams would also play in October, when Brown returned to Cleveland. But the November date in this new intrastate rivalry excited everyone.

But before the first kickoff, things went kerflooey. Cook had injured his throwing arm during the previous season. It seemed to be one of those injuries that would heal over time. But when he reported for training camp at Wilmington, Ohio, the soreness was still there and getting worse. It was actually a torn rotator cuff, and it had been misdiagnosed and mistreated. The arm was hurt beyond repair, and Cook would join the long, melancholy list of football's what-ifs. His brilliant career was effectively over.

Then comes one of the strange turns of fate that makes the game such a joy.

The Bengals had to bring in Virgil Carter as an emergency replacement. Carter had spent a few years with the Bears after graduating from Brigham Young University, one of the first to come out of that quarterback factory. His physical gifts were limited, especially when it came to the long passing attack that had been designed for Cook. But Carter was a highly accurate short passer and understood the game thoroughly. He was cast in the mold of another Brown favorite: the brainy star he groomed in Cleveland, Frank Ryan. Carter attended business school to get a postgraduate degree, and he also taught statistics at Xavier University in Cincinnati.

So Brown and Walsh went to work with him and drew up the first incarnation of the West Coast offense. Carter was no Joe Montana, but he got the idea. With Trumpy, Eric Crabtree, and Chip Myers as his receivers, the coaches thought Carter could make it work.

But not smoothly and not right away. In the first game ever played at Riverfront, the Bengals managed to knock off the perennially strong Oakland Raiders, 31–21, with Sam Wyche as the quarterback.

Then things went bad in a hurry. There were consecutive thumpings by Detroit and Houston. Then the Bengals were headed for Cleveland and the first of the two much-anticipated meetings between these Ohio teams.

However, it was not really their first meeting. They had played an exhibition game in August in Cleveland, but no one had paid much attention to that. The Bengals scrubs defeated the Browns rookies. But this one was for keeps.

"I believe the Bengals will be fired up...for a lot of reasons," said Blanton Collier, now in his eighth year as the Cleveland coach.

But Brown dismissed it as "just another game." Or then again, maybe not.

"We are trying to build something," Brown said. "From the start, people in Ohio wanted to know 'Can you beat the Browns?' That's the team they had known and could identify with professional football. We were dealt a tremendous artistic blow when Cook was lost, but we set our minds to do the best we can.

"People forget that I've been away from Cleveland for eight years. I've only been downtown once since I left. I left a lot of my life there."

He had to pause at that point to compose himself, wrote Tom Place, *The Plain Dealer* reporter.

"It's hard to believe," Brown went on after a moment, "that Katy will be gone two years next spring.

"But bitter people bore me. People who tell you their troubles. I've made an effort after my tragedies not to talk about them."

But Brown was being more than a bit disingenuous. The bitterness he harbored toward Modell hadn't abated a bit. The years only seemed to make it burn more intensely.

As it turned out, the Browns won a very tight game, 30–27, with two touchdowns in the fourth quarter. Cincinnati had rallied behind Carter, who was making his first start of the season, to come within a field goal. But Cleveland managed to run out the clock and take the victory.

The Browns presented the game ball to Modell, and Brown was booed by the Cleveland crowd when he left the field without shaking hands with Collier.

"I haven't shaken the other coach's hands after a game for years," he explained, tampering down speculation that there was antagonism between him and his successor. "Blanton knows this. You never know when someone is going to come out and take a swing at you. It should be eliminated. I went up to him before the game, and we did our socializing then."

Some reporters thought the Cincinnati uniforms resembled those of the Browns so closely that "it could have been an intrasquad game." Both teams also ran fairly identical offensive schemes—unavoidable when two coaches who had been associated with each other for so long were meeting.

The effect was heightened when Brown remarked, "I was proud of the Browns."

Some reporters thought they'd heard him wrong or that Brown had made an embarrassing slip of the tongue.

"No, they showed poise out there," he said. "You have to admire that."

Otto Graham stopped by the locker room to wish his old coach well. So did Dante Lavelli, Tommy James, and Tony Adamle. The old flame still burned among the original Browns.

But that was mere sentiment. What mattered most was that Carter moved the ball well. What's more, he said that he actually liked the messenger guards.

"The coaches did a tremendous job of translating my skills to the situation," he said.

It looked like the start of a beautiful friendship.

But the Bengals were 1–3 with the loss, and things did not get better. Three more losses followed, and halfway through the season Cincinnati was a doleful 1–6. The year was clearly a washout, and even a 43–14 pasting of Buffalo on the road wasn't going to change that.

Then it was time for the Browns again. The AFC Central was weak in 1970, and at 4–4 for the year, Cleveland was in the lead. It did not appear that Cincinnati was a serious threat.

Collier warned that Carter had settled comfortably into the Browns system. Trumpy, who hadn't played in Cleveland, was healthy again and was a force at tight end for the Bengals.

Moreover, Bill Nelsen, who had engineered the win in Cleveland, was hurt, and the Browns were going with a rookie, Mike Phipps. Phipps had been their top draft pick and played well in an earlier victory at Pittsburgh. But he was still a rookie, and he would be stepping into a cauldron of hysteria.

The biggest crowd in Cincinnati history, more than 60,000 fans, came out for the rematch. During Brown's big years in Cleveland, the

Indians were also winning, and one sport seemed to feed off the other to enhance the excitement.

So it was in Cincinnati. Sparky Anderson had taken the Reds to the World Series in his first year as manager. The team became known as the Big Red Machine, and it had kept Riverfront Stadium jumping all summer. They eventually went down to the Baltimore Orioles, but the lingering buzz was transferred to the Bengals. Everyone in town wanted to be at this grudge match.

The game turned out to be a contest of wills. Leroy Kelly burst in from eight yards out on Cleveland's fifth play from scrimmage at the end of a 77-yard march. Then the Browns recovered a fumble on the Bengals' 20 and seemed ready to break it open. The Bengals argued strenuously that the play was an incomplete pass, not a lateral. But the decision stood.

The Cincinnati defense was aroused, though, and stopped the Browns short of a first down. A field goal made it 10–0. But something had changed in the tide of this game, and the Browns would get just 150 yards in total offense the rest of the way.

Carter finally began moving the team. The Bengals came downfield right after the following kickoff, and he hit Phillips on a 13-yard touchdown pass.

In the third quarter, they returned for more. This time it was an 85-yard march, with Robinson going in from the 1. Cincinnai had the lead, 14–10. And that was it. It was now a matter of ball control. There would be no more scoring.

The Bengals knew that Cleveland had a great pass rush and had prepared a series of running plays for Carter. He ended up as the top rusher in the game, with 110 yards, and his legs kept one drive after another alive. He never allowed the Browns to take over with any kind of field position.

When the gun sounded, Brown took off his hat, leaped in the air, whirled around a few times, and then dashed for the dressing room.

"Paul Brown Gets Football Revenge," read the headlines in the Cleveland papers. They got that right.

For all his talk of having no bitterness, Brown wanted this game more than any other he had ever coached. He immediately labeled it "my greatest victory." Players said later that he had wept when he congratulated the team.

By the time reporters were allowed in, the mood was still raucous in the Bengals' clubhouse. Brown's players didn't have to be told what this game meant to their coach.

"We knew how badly he wanted it," said Bergey.

His players gave him the game ball.

"Satisfied," Brown said. "That's how I feel. Just like Bill Willis used to say. Satisfied. This victory makes coming back worthwhile. I wanted this so badly. I feel like an 18-year-old kid. It's like winning the Super Bowl for these kids."

In a corner of the locker room he spotted some reporters from the Canton-Massillon area. "I guess some people up in your territory will like this," he called to them—overlooking the fact that his old training ground was well within Browns country.

But the Browns were no longer Ohio's team. That's what this victory had accomplished, and Brown knew it well. His Bengals had been placed on an even footing with the long-established franchise. It would now be a true rivalry, splitting the state in half.

"Undoubtedly it was humiliating for Modell and Collier to lose to Paul Brown's team," wrote Lebovitz. "There are no alibis. They deserved the victory. They were a superior club and a superior coach."

The circle had come around.

15

The Long Good-bye

On New Year's Day 1976, a time for fresh beginnings, Paul Brown called the public relations director of the Bengals at his home, told him that he was stepping down as coach, and directed him to put out a press release to that effect. He would continue as the team's general manager and run the front office, but after 45 years he was off the sidelines for good. That part of his career was finished.

It was 13 years, almost to the day, since he had been garroted by Art Modell. The clear implication had been that he was a fossil, hopelessly left behind by the game he had transformed.

No one could argue that way anymore.

"It was totally Paul's decision," said the team's majority stockholder, John Sawyer. "He notified me a few days before that he might do something like this, but he wasn't absolutely sure. He just decided he wanted to let somebody else do it."

No one else in the organization had an inkling. But there had been rumors. It was known the 49ers were after Bill Johnson as their head coach. Brown was carefully grooming him as his successor and didn't want to lose him. So that factor played into the decision, too. Among others.

Even though Brown was now 67 years old, his decision still was described as a "thunderbolt announcement" in the newspapers. It was front-page news across Ohio. *The Plain Dealer* editorialized about it under the headline "Builder Brown."

"More than any other person, he made professional football respectable," said the top paper in the city Brown felt had turned its back on him. "He gave it a first-class image. He insisted that everyone, from players to league officials, demonstrate maturity and stability. He took it from a ragtag organization to systematic responsibility."

He had, indeed, done all that. And now there was nothing left to prove.

After the landmark win over Cleveland in 1970, the Bengals had gone on and won their last five games. Before another record Riverfront crowd they pummeled the Patriots in the season finale, 45–7, and with an 8–6 record went into the playoffs.

In only three years, Brown had taken a brand-new team into the NFL postseason. It was, at that time, an unmatched accomplishment. He was the miracle man again. No other football team had reached such a high level so quickly. The mark would not be equaled until 1996, when both Jacksonville and Carolina reached the playoffs in their second seasons.

The Bengals were blanked at Baltimore, 17–0, in the playoff game. But even that couldn't diminish the luster of the season. When the Colts went on to win the Super Bowl, even that slight sting was diminished.

It appeared that Carter's mastery of the control passing offense was about to elevate Cincinnati to the elite ranks. But it wasn't to be that easy.

As the rest of the league began to realize the limitations of his long passing game, they began stacking defenses to stop him. Cincinnati's runners were not credible enough to give him another option. Then he hurt his shoulder in the third game of the 1971 season and had to sit out four weeks.

After smashing the Eagles in the opener, the team went on to lose seven straight games. Unlike the previous year, it could not recover from this losing streak. Cincinnati finished at 4–10, far out of the play-offs. What made it seem worse was that the Bengals were in almost every game they played. Six of their losses were by four points or fewer, including both games with the Browns. Carter's final stats were good, but the team was acquiring the rap of being unable to win the close ones. It appeared that Brown was back to square one in Cincinnati.

But the future had already arrived. It had come on the 1971 college draft day.

The Bengals had taken linemen with their first two picks. But the player Brown really had his eye on was still available in the third round.

He knew that Norm Van Brocklin had scouted this player for Atlanta and was going to choose him soon. Brown had sweated it out as long as he could. So with the team's third pick, the 67th of the draft, the Bengals selected Ken Anderson of Augustana College.

Only a few insiders recognized the name, and fewer than that had ever heard of Augustana. The small private school played a Division III schedule in the College Conference of Illinois and Wisconsin. In its class, it is recognized as a good small college organization. But its class seldom, if ever, sends quarterbacks to the NFL.

Yet every report Brown had received on him from Walsh and Mike Brown rated Anderson as an outstanding prospect. Besides, in this era of eroding values, Anderson seemed to be exactly the sort of Midwestern kid with his head screwed on straight Brown always had admired. The kind of kid Cook was. And like Otto Graham.

Losing Cook had been a crushing disappointment, especially after it became apparent that Carter would be no more than a temporary answer. So the Bengals rolled the dice and came up with the greatest star in their history.

His greatness would have been hard to guess at the start. Brown did not relish rushing young quarterbacks into starting roles, but when Carter went down and with Cook still unable to play, he had no choice.

Anderson first went into a game against Green Bay after Carter was hurt. Brown said Anderson mistakenly cut inside on a fake field goal run instead of going for the corner and was tackled short of the end zone. Bengals lose, 20–17.

Two weeks later an 11-point lead to Cleveland evaporated. Bengals lose, 27–24.

The week after that, George Blanda brought Oakland back in the last minute. Bengals lose, 31–27.

And the week after that, Anderson had a hip pointer but was still the only quarterback healthy enough to start against Houston. Bengals lose, 10–6.

Of the five games he played, the Bengals had been close in every one but a 10-point drubbing by Miami, the team that would go on to the Super Bowl. But the Bengals had lost them all.

If Anderson thought he'd get credit for a nice try, he was quickly disabused of that notion.

"Well, Anderson," said the coach at the film session after the Houston game. "This is the fourth game you've lost for us now."

But this was only Brown's version of tough love. Although Carter returned as the starting quarterback the following week, Brown had seen enough. The Bengals went into the 1972 season with Anderson as the unquestioned starter. Brown described him as "the quarterback we had been waiting for," the man who could take up the mantle of the incomparable Graham.

Milt Plum and Jim Ninowski had been bitter disappointments. Frank Ryan may have been the answer, but Brown was out of Cleveland before he reached his peak. Cook could have gone on to greatness were it not for his ruined shoulder. Virgil Carter was tremendously bright but with a limited arm. But Anderson...here, at last, was the complete package: smart, disciplined, physically gifted, and with all the leadership intangibles.

The learning process continued. The Bengals started out at 4–1 in 1972 and won three out of their last four games. But in the middle they were 1–4, and that was enough to keep them from the playoffs.

The breakout season came in 1973. Anderson threw 18 touchdown passes. The revamped running attack featured Essex Johnson and rookie Boobie Clark, and both of them rushed for more than 900 yards. Another rookie, Isaac Curtis, turned into one of the greatest deep threats in the league. The defense shut out Minnesota, which would go on to the Super Bowl, and held Buffalo's O.J. Simpson to fewer than 100 yards. (This was the season Simpson ran for more than 2,000— the record at that time.)

The Bengals won their last six in a row, finished 10-4, and made the playoffs for the second time. But they were matched against one of the greatest teams of all time, the defending champion Miami Dolphins. Cincinnati stayed in it for 30 minutes, but an injury to Johnson bottled up the rushing game. Miami drew away in the second half to win 34-16.

Again, however, the team seemed primed for great things.

Life was also growing brighter on a personal level for Brown. All three of his sons—Mike, Pete, and Robin—were working with the Bengals in some capacity. Brown had remarried in 1973. His new wife had come to work for him as a secretary after she had been widowed, and the office romance blossomed. The coach who had been the father only of sons even enjoyed having two teenaged daughters in the house with his new family.

But the roller-coaster ride for the team continued in 1974. Again it got off to a quick 4-1 start, and then one after another the Bengals went down to injuries. Both Johnson and Clark were out of the lineup. Cincinnati was never able to mount a running game to match Anderson's leading the league in passing. Finally, even he went down with an injury. The team lost four of its last five games, finished 7-7, and sat home for the playoffs again.

Then it finally came together.

By 1975 the Bengals were a formidable, veteran team. Anderson, already acknowledged as one of the most accurate passers in the game, outdid even his own standard, completing more than 60 percent of his throws.

Curtis and Charlie Joyner were outstanding deep threats. Clark was the team's leading rusher and also turned into the possession receiver that was essential to any Brown-designed offense. Clark compiled 928 all-purpose yards.

Rookie halfback Stan Fritts became a goal-line specialist, leading the team with eight touchdowns. Fritts combined with Lenvil Elliott to add 683 yards to the running game. Center Bob Johnson, one of the original Bengals, anchored the offensive line.

Even though defensive tackle Mike Reid had retired to pursue a career as a classical pianist, Cincinnati presented a smart, quick defense. Lemar Parrish was an All-Pro cornerback, and his partners, Ken Riley and Bernard Jackson, picked off 11 passes.

The Bengals could match up against any team in the NFL, with the sole exception of the Pittsburgh Steelers. Unfortunately, they were in the same division. Only in four games did the Bengals give up as many as three touchdowns. Two of them, however, were against Pittsburgh, and Cincinnati lost both times.

Just as with Don Shula's Miami and Don McCafferty's Baltimore team, when competing against Pittsburgh, Brown was running up against a coach who had grown up in his system and applied all the things he had learned against the teacher. Chuck Noll had been part of the Browns championship era, and his Steelers were in the midst of winning four Super Bowls in six years with the Steel Curtain defense.

The Bengals finished 11–3, the best mark in their history. But it was only good for a wild-card berth in the playoffs. They were matched against Oakland, a team they had beaten 14–10 during the season. But that was at Riverfront. Because they were the wild-card, the rematch would be at the Oakland Coliseum.

The Raiders broke ahead early, with Ken Stabler picking apart the Bengals defense and the Oakland front forcing Anderson to throw in a hurry. It was 31–14 in the fourth quarter before the Bengals suddenly caught fire.

Riley picked off Stabler's only interception of the day, and Anderson hit Joiner for a 25-yard touchdown. Minutes later, Curtis made a leaping catch in the end zone, and now it was 31–28 with five minutes to go.

Stabler then fumbled at his own 37. All at once, the Bengals were looking at a highly unlikely win. But on first down, Anderson was thrown for his fifth loss of the day, and the team could never get close enough to go for the tying field goal.

Once more the Bengals were eliminated from the playoffs in the first round.

The game was played on December 28. Four days later, Brown announced that he was through with coaching.

In his autobiography, he said that as he stood on the sidelines, he knew this could be his last game. If it were, he would walk away with no regrets. And that's exactly what happened.

The chance that the Bengals might lose his hand-picked successor fed into Brown's decision. But there was much more.

His career had spanned 45 years, through cultural and technological changes unimaginable when he began, from Rudy Vallee to Elton John and from Clark Gable to Tiny Tim. The contrast doesn't get more vivid than that.

He had watched boys he had coached become old men. He had seen players he had mentored turn into giants of the coaching profession. His disciples won seven of the 10 Super Bowls of the 1970s, and Walsh would add three more in the 1980s. He had seen a game he loved for its pure competition utterly transformed by the allure of big money—in his mind, not for better.

Brown had come into professional football with a new league and signed up the players he wanted by giving them checks. Still, he professed to be puzzled by all the emphasis on money in the 1970s, by threats from some of his players to jump to the new World Football League, by union hardball tactics.

He had been a part of the sport's transformation through organization, strategy, and stability. He did not understand what drove a man like Art Modell, and he never would.

When he wrote his autobiography four years later with Jack Clary, he included this passage:

> Art was not a football person. I resented his lack of
> background in the football world and did not respect
> his knowledge, and I probably showed it many times,
> not helping the situation any.... The relationship

between the two of us has been described as a personality conflict, but it was much more than that. It was a
basic conflict between two different styles and two different philosophies of operating—one from knowledge
and experience, the other from a complete lack of
either.

This rancorous comment was from a man who had told reporters
before the first Bengals-Browns game in 1970 that he had no patience
for bitterness.

Modell complained about that passage to Pete Rozelle, and Brown
ended up being fined $10,000 for this appraisal of the man who had
fired him.

The front cover of Brown's book had a photograph of him being
carried off the field by a group of Cincinnati players. The back cover
showed him in a Bengals cap. Nothing was there of the Browns.

He claimed that he had never lost his zeal for coaching. But he also
understood that he was now a man in late middle age with an energy
level that was not what it once had been. He loved Anderson, but many
of the younger players came from backgrounds that were alien to him
and brought attitudes he could not fathom. He could not stand the
touchdown dances and the other acts of exhibitionism.

"Act like you've been there before," he told the end-zone cavorters.

The media had changed, too. Gone were the writers who believed
in getting behind their teams and writing positive stories. What was so
wrong with that? Now it seemed to him that the rippers had carried the
day and were only probing for the negative slant.

Maybe the game hadn't passed him by. Maybe the country had.

As general manager, he could deal with the players as abstractions.
There were few sharper judges of talent in the game. Time had not
eroded his ability as a builder.

It would take another five years, though, before the Bengals reached
the Super Bowl. By that time, Johnson had been fired as coach, and
Forrest Gregg took over.

Anderson would be around to lead them to the championship. Curtis, Riley, and linebacker Jim LeClair, all of whom had played for Brown, would still be starters. So would players he had selected in his final draft as coach—linebackers Glenn Cameron and Bo Harris and punter Pat McInally.

It had taken 13 years to get there, and although the Bengals lost to San Francisco, at least they made it to the big game. That was more than could be said for the Browns. Despite several excellent years, they never played in the Super Bowl.

Modell watched in mounting anger as Cleveland committed itself to a new baseball stadium for the Indians and a new basketball arena for the Cavaliers. Didn't these politicians understand that the Browns were the moneymakers? They had chained him to a windy relic of a stadium—uncomfortable, outmoded, and unsuited for the profitable frills that team owners now saw as an urgent need.

The Browns only had to open the gates, and 70,000 people would pour into the old stadium. Modell swore that come what may he would never betray that support and move the Browns. But in 1995, he did. The Cleveland Browns became the Baltimore Ravens, and the name and history of a proud franchise were obliterated.

Modell became the most reviled man in Cleveland. He received hate mail, death threats, unprintable postcards. For a long time, he didn't dare appear in public in the city. Longtime friends stopped speaking to him. The Browns alumni mourned, and many of them wept. Even Jim Brown, perhaps forgetting the role he had played, indicated that if Modell would fire Paul Brown—"and that was like firing God"—he was certainly capable of moving the team.

The NFL, however, recognized the injustice of the move and awarded Cleveland an expansion franchise for the 1999 season. There was no argument about naming it the Browns.

Paul Brown didn't live to see the team he founded trashed by the man he despised.

He continued in the Bengals front office, deliberately avoiding the spotlight. He had never truly enjoyed the glare of publicity but recognized that it was one of the duties of a coach. Now that was no longer necessary. He was content to be the gray eminence, behind the scenes, putting the pieces together, a dry martini before dinner, some Artie Shaw on the stereo.

Sometimes he would drive back to Massillon, visit Katy's grave, and sit in front of the stadium he had helped to build. It was now named for him. He thought that was a wonderful honor.

There was always another winner to build, and in 1988 the Bengals reached the Super Bowl again. Boomer Esiason was not quite the disciplined sort of quarterback that Brown liked, but that year he got the job done. In the week before the game, however, Brown's worst nightmare came true. The Bengals' top runner, Stanley Wilson, was arrested by Miami police on drug possession charges and was suspended for the Super Bowl.

It was everything the coach had always warned against, why he gave the same old speech at the start of every season. It was why he had thrown the team captain off his Browns for driving under the influence before the 1946 championship game. Brown had always prided himself in making sure that his teams did things the right way. It was what he stood for, his credo. Now it had turned to ashes.

And when Joe Montana threw the winning touchdown pass with 34 seconds left in the game to deny the Bengals again, it was almost too much.

Two and a half years later, on August 5, 1991, Brown passed away at his home of complications from pneumonia. He was 83 years old and had been off the sidelines for 15 seasons. With diminished visibility, the memory already was starting to fade.

"He always said that playing good football meant being in the spirit of the occasion," recalled Anderson. "If you played well and lost, you could walk off the field holding your head high. He never believed in the Vince Lombardi quote about 'winning was the only thing.' He believed that making the effort to win was the only thing."

Other players recalled how he had gone out of his way to find them jobs, instructed them to regard football as a stepping stone and not an end in itself. The image of the ogre, the feared critic of the Wednesday morning game movies (Brown always called them movies, never films), was receding.

Weeb Ewbank recalled when he went to work for Brown as an assistant in Cleveland: "He told me to coach the tackles. I said, 'Paul, I played quarterback.' But he knew I'd have to work very hard at this job and bring a fresh approach. That's how his mind worked."

The New York Times sports columnist Ira Berkow wrote this description of him: "He was known as a mechanical man, unsmiling, robot-like. If he didn't exactly invent Xs and Os, at least he expanded and refined them. And when you saw him prowling the sidelines in his long winter coat...he looked like my idea of Digger O'Dell, the undertaker on the radio show *Life of Riley*."

Maybe the best epitaph was written by Chuck Heaton, the writer for *The* (Cleveland) *Plain Dealer*, upon Brown's retirement.

"All of football is better," Heaton wrote, "for his having been a coach."

Brown was buried in Massillon, coming home at last to stay.

It is hard to assess exactly how much Paul Brown meant to the Bengals in the years after he gave up coaching. It is significant to note, however, that in the decade following his death, the Bengals had the worst record of any team in the NFL.

But in 2000 Cincinnati opened a new football-only facility on its riverfront and dedicated it with the hope that its link to the past would bring better days for the Bengals.

It was named Paul Brown Stadium.

APPENDIX

Complete Coaching Record

1930: Severn School
Tome 7-6
Loyola 6-0
Forest Park 20-0
Baltimore Poly 14-12
McDonough 12-7
Mt. St. Joseph 26-0
St. James win, no score
available

Season: 7-0-0
Points scored: 85,
opponents 25 (minus
St. James game)

1930: Severn School
Calvert Hall 0-13
Tome 6-0
Loyola 0-6
Forest Park 33-7
Baltimore Poly 14-0
McDonough 14-13
Mt. St. Joseph 0-0
St. James 18-6

Season: 5-2-1
Points scored: Severn 85,
opponents 45

**1932: Massillon
Washington High
School**
Wooster 20-7
Akron East 7-6
Niles McKinley 8-0
Akron South 12-6
New Philadelphia 26-0

Barberton 0-0
Alliance 6-30
Warren Harding 0-12
Dover 0-18
Canton McKinley 0-19

Season: 5-4-1
Points scored: Massillon
79, opponents 98

**1933: Massillon
Washington High
School**
Akron St. Vincent 39-0
Niles McKinley 13-0
Wooster 53-0
New Philadelphia 70-0
Barberton 0-6
Alliance 19-0
Columbus Aquinas 52-6
Akron East 25-0
Tiffin 40-19
Canton McKinley 0-21

Season: 8-2
Points scored: Massillon
311, opponents 52

**1934: Massillon
Washington High
School**
Tiffin 37-0
Cleveland Shaw 46-0
Sharon, Pennsylvania
27-0
Youngstown South 45-0
Barberton 54-0

Alliance 65-0
Akron West 33-0
Akron East 42-0
Niles McKinley 72-0
Canton McKinley 6-21

Season: 9-1
Points scored: Massillon
427, opponents 21

**1935: Massillon
Washington High
School**
Akron East 70-0
Cleveland Shaw 66-0
Portsmouth 46-0
Youngstown South 64-0
Barberton 34-0
Alliance 27-0
Akron West 52-7
New Philadelphia 65-0
Niles McKinley 53-6
Canton McKinley 6-0

Season: 10-0
Points scored: Massillon
483, opponents 13

**1936: Massillon
Washington
High School**
Cleveland East 58-0
Mansfield 40-7
Portsmouth 70-0
Akron South 57-0
New Castle, Pennsylvania
13-0

Alliance 51–0
Akron North 46–0
Columbus East 52–0
Barberton 35–7
Canton McKinley 21–0

Season: 10–0
Points scored: Massillon
443, opponents 14

**1937: Massillon
Washington
High School**
Horace Mann, Indiana
33–13
Mansfield 6–6
Warren Harding 23–6
Cedar Rapids, Iowa 39–0
Alliance 39–6
Steubenville Wells 13–0
New Castle, Pennsylvania
0–7
Youngstown Chaney 28–6
Barberton 28–0
Canton McKinley 19–6

Season: 8–1–1
Points scored: Massillon
228, opponents 50

**1938: Massillon
Washington
High School**
McKeesport, Pennsylvania
19–7
Mansfield 33–7
Warren Harding 21–0
Sharon, Pennsylvania
37–20
Alliance 19–6
Steubenville Wells 31–0
New Castle, Pennsylvania
52–7
Canton Lehman 52–0
Youngstown Chaney 26–13
Canton McKinley 12–0

Season: 10–0
Points scored: Massillon
302, opponents 60

**1939: Massillon
Washington
High School**
Cleveland Cathedral Latin
40–13
Mansfield 73–0
Warren Harding 33–0
Erie, Pennsylvania, East
66–0
Alliance 47–0
Steubenville Wells 50–0
New Castle, Pennsylvania
46–0
Canton Lehman 47–6
Youngstown Chaney 38–0
Canton McKinley 20–6

Season: 10–0
Points scored: Massillon
460, opponents 25

**1940: Massillon
Washington
High School**
Cleveland Cathedral Latin
64–0
Weirton, West Virginia
48–0
Warren Harding 59–0
Erie, Pennsylvania, East
74–0
Alliance 40–0
Steubenville Wells 66–0
Mansfield 38–0
Toledo Waite 28–0
Youngstown East 26–0
Canton McKinley 34–6

Season: 10–0
Points scored: Massillon
477, opponents 6

**1941: Ohio State
University**
Missouri 12–7
Southern California 33–0
Purdue 16–14
Northwestern 7–14
Pittsburgh 21–14
Wisconsin 46–34

Illinois 12–7
Michigan 20–20

Season: 6–1–1
Points scored: Ohio State
167, opponents 110

**1942: Ohio State
University**
Fort Knox 59–0
Indiana 32–21
Southern California 28–12
Purdue 26–0
Northwestern 20–6
Wisconsin 7–17
Pittsburgh 59–19
Illinois 44–20
Michigan 21–7
Iowa Pre-Flight 41–12

Season: 9–1
Points scored: Ohio State
337, opponents 114

**1943: Ohio State
University**
Iowa Pre-Flight 13–28
Missouri 27–6
Great Lakes 6–13
Purdue 7–30
Northwestern 0–13
Indiana 14–20
Pittsburgh 46–6
Illinois 29–26
Michigan 7–45

Season: 3–6
Points scored: Ohio State
149, opponents 187

**1944: Great Lakes
Fort Sheridan 62–0**
Purdue 27–18
Illinois 26–26
Northwestern 25–0
Western Michigan 38–0
Ohio State 6–26
Wisconsin 40–12
Marquette 45–7
Morris Field 12–10

Marquette 32–0
Fort Warren 28–7
Notre Dame 7–28

Season: 9–2–1
Points scored: Great Lakes
348, opponents 134

**1945: Great Lakes
College
All-Stars 0–35**
Michigan 2–27
Wisconsin 0–0
Purdue 6–20
Fort Benning 12–21
Marquette 37–27
Western Michigan 39–0
Illinois 12–6
Michigan State 27–7
Fort Warren 47–14
Notre Dame 39–7

Season: 6–4–1
Points scored: Great Lakes
221, opponents 164

**1946: Cleveland Browns
(AAFC)**
Miami 44–0
Chicago 20–6
Buffalo 28–0
New York 24–7
Brooklyn 26–7
New York 7–0
Los Angeles 31–14
San Francisco 20–34
Los Angeles 16–17
San Francisco 14–7
Chicago 51–14
Buffalo 42–17
Miami 34–0
Brooklyn 66–14

Season: 12–2
Points scored: Cleveland
423, opponents 137
Championship: Cleveland
14, New York 9

**1947: Cleveland Browns
(AAFC)**
Buffalo 30–14
Brooklyn 55–7
Baltimore 28–0
Chicago 41–21
New York 26–17
Los Angeles 10–13
Chicago 31–28
San Francisco 14–7
Buffalo 28–7
Brooklyn 13–12
San Francisco 37–14
New York 28–28
Los Angeles 27–17
Baltimore 42–0

Season: 12–1–1
Points scored: Cleveland
410, opponents 185
Championship: Cleveland
14, New York 3

**1948: Cleveland Browns
(AAFC)**
Los Angeles 19–14
Buffalo 42–13
Chicago 28–7
Chicago 21–10
Baltimore 14–10
Brooklyn 30–17
Buffalo 31–14
New York 35–7
Baltimore 28–7
San Francisco 14–7
New York 34–21
Los Angeles 31–14
San Francisco 31–28
Brooklyn 31–21

Season: 14–0–0
Points scored: Cleveland
389, opponents 190
Championship: Cleveland
49, Buffalo 7

**1949: Cleveland Browns
(AAFC)**
Buffalo 28–28
Baltimore 21–0

New York 14–3
Baltimore 28–20
Los Angeles 42–7
San Francisco 28–56
Los Angeles 61–14
San Francisco 30–28
Chicago 35–2
Buffalo 7–7
New York 31–0
Chicago 14–6

Season: 9–1–2
Points scored: Cleveland
339, opponents 171
Playoff: Cleveland 31,
Buffalo 21
Championship: Cleveland
21, San Francisco 7

**1950: Cleveland Browns
(NFL)**
Philadelphia 35–10
Baltimore 31–0
New York Giants 0–6
Pittsburgh 30–17
Chicago Cardinals 34–24
New York Giants 13–17
Pittsburgh 45–7
Chicago Cardinals 10–7
San Francisco 34–14
Washington 20–14
Philadelphia 13–7
Washington 45–21

Season: 10–2
Points scored: Cleveland
310, opponents 144
Playoff: Cleveland 8, New
York Giants 3
Championship: Cleveland
30, Los Angeles 28

**1951: Cleveland Browns
(NFL)**
San Francisco 10–24
Los Angeles 38–23
Washington 45–0
Pittsburgh 17–0
New York Giants 14–13
Chicago Cardinals 34–17

207

Philadelphia 20–17
New York Giants 10–0
Chicago Bears 42–21
Chicago Cardinals 49–28
Pittsburgh 28–0
Philadelphia 24–9

Season: 11–1–0
Points scored: Cleveland
331, opponents 152
Championship: Los
Angeles 24, Cleveland 17

1952: Cleveland Browns (NFL)
Los Angeles 37–7
Pittsburgh 21–20
New York Giants 9–17
Philadelphia 49–7
Washington 19–15
Detroit 6–17
Chicago Cardinals 28–13
Pittsburgh 29–28
Philadelphia 20–28
Washington 48–24
Chicago Cardinals 10–0
New York Giants 34–37

Season: 8–4
Points scored: Cleveland
310, opponents 213
Championship: Detroit 17,
Cleveland 7

1953: Cleveland Browns (NFL)
Green Bay 27–0
Chicago Cardinals 27–7
Philadelphia 37–13
Washington 30–14
New York Giants 7–0
Washington 27–3
Pittsburgh 34–16
San Francisco 23–21
Pittsburgh 20–16
Chicago Cardinals 27–16
New York Giants 62–14
Philadelphia 27–42

Season: 11–1
Points scored: Cleveland
348, opponents 162
Championship: Detroit 17,
Cleveland 16

1954: Cleveland Browns (NFL)
Philadelphia 10–28
Chicago Cardinals 31–7
Pittsburgh 27–55
Chicago Cardinals 35–3
New York Giants 24–14
Washington 62–3
Chicago Bears 39–10
Philadelphia 6–0
New York Giants 16–7
Washington 34–14
Pittsburgh 42–7
Detroit 10–14

Season: 9–3
Points scored: Cleveland
336, opponents 162
Championship: Cleveland
56, Detroit 10

1955: Cleveland Browns (NFL)
Washington 17–27
San Francisco 38–3
Philadelphia 21–17
Washington 24–14
Green Bay 41–10
Chicago Cardinals 26–20
New York Giants 24–14
Philadelphia 17–33
Pittsburgh 41–14
New York Giants 35–35
Pittsburgh 30–7
Chicago Cardinals 35–24
Season: 9–2–1
Points scored: Cleveland
349, opponents 218
Championship: Cleveland
38, Los Angeles 14

1956: Cleveland Browns (NFL)
Chicago Cardinals 7–9
Pittsburgh 14–10
New York Giants 9–21
Washington 9–20
Pittsburgh 16–24
Green Bay 24–7
Baltimore 7–21
Philadelphia 16–0
Washington 17–20
Philadelphia 17–14
New York Giants 24–7
Chicago Cardinals 7–24

Season: 5–7
Points scored: Cleveland
167, opponents 177
Championship: Cleveland
167, opponents 177

1957: Cleveland Browns (NFL)
New York Giants 6–0
Pittsburgh 23–12
Philadelphia 24–7
Philadelphia 7–17
Chicago Cardinals 17–7
Washington 21–17
Pittsburgh 24–0
Washington 30–30
Los Angeles 45–31
Chicago Cardinals 31–0
Detroit 7–20
New York Giants 34–28

Season: 9–2–1
Points scored: Cleveland
269, opponents 172
Championship: Detroit 59,
Cleveland 14

1958: Cleveland Browns (NFL)
Los Angeles 30–27
Pittsburgh 45–12
Chicago Cardinals 35–28
Pittsburgh 27–10
Chicago Cardinals 38–24

New York Giants 17–21
Detroit 10–30
Washington 20–10
Philadelphia 28–14
Washington 21–14
Philadelphia 21–14
New York Giants 10–13

Season: 9–3
Points scored: Cleveland
302, opponents 217
Playoff: Giants 10,
Cleveland 0
Championship: New York
Giants 10, Cleveland 0

1959: Cleveland Browns (NFL)
Pittsburgh 7–17
Chicago Cardinals 34–7
Giants 6–10
Chicago Cardinals 17–7
Washington 34–7
Baltimore 38–31
Philadelphia 28–7
Washington 31–17
Pittsburgh 20–21
San Francisco 20–21
New York Giants 7–48
Philadelphia 28–21

Season: 7–5
Points scored: Cleveland
270, opponents 214

1960: Cleveland Browns (NFL)
Philadelphia 41–24
Pittsburgh 28–20
Dallas 48–7
Philadelphia 29–31
Washington 31–10
New York Giants 13–17
St. Louis 28–27
Pittsburgh 10–14
St. Louis 17–17
Washington 27–16
Chicago 42–0
New York Giants 48–34

Season: 8–3–1
Points scored: Cleveland
362, opponents 217
Playoff: Detroit 17,
Cleveland 16

1961: Cleveland Browns (NFL)
Philadelphia 20–27
St. Louis 20–17
Dallas 25–7
Washington 31–7
Green Bay 17–49
Pittsburgh 30–28
St. Louis 21–10
Pittsburgh 13–17
Washington 17–6
Philadelphia 45–24
New York Giants 21–37
Dallas 38–17
Chicago 14–17
New York Giants 7–7

Season: 8–5–1
Points scored: Cleveland
319, opponents 270

1962: Cleveland Browns (NFL)
New York Giants 17–7
Washington 16–17
Philadelphia 7–35
Dallas 19–10
Baltimore 14–36
St. Louis 34–7
Pittsburgh 41–14
Philadelphia 14–14
Washington 9–17
St. Louis 38–14
Pittsburgh 35–14
Dallas 21–45
New York Giants 13–17
San Francisco 13–10

Season: 7–6–1
Points scored: Cleveland
291, opponents 257

1968: Cincinnati Bengals (AFL)
San Diego 13–29
Denver 24–10
Buffalo 34–23
San Diego 10–31
Denver 7–10
Kansas City 3–13
Miami 22–24
Oakland 10–31
Houston 17–27
Kansas City 9–16
Miami 38–21
Oakland 0–34
Boston 14–33
New York Jets 14–27

Season: 3–11
Points scored: Bengals 215,
opponents 329

1969: Cincinnati Bengals (AFL)
Miami 27–21
San Diego 34–20
Kansas City 24–19
San Diego 14–21
New York Jets 7–21
Denver 23–30
Kansas City 22–42
Oakland 31–17
Houston 31–31
Boston 14–25
New York Jets 7–40
Buffalo 13–16
Oakland 17–37
Denver 16–27

Season: 4–9–1
Points scored: Bengals 280,
opponents 367

1970: Cincinnati Bengals (NFL)
Oakland 31–21
Detroit 3–38
Houston 13–20
Cleveland 27–30
Kansas City 19–27

Washington 0–20
Pittsburgh 10–21
Buffalo 43–14
Cleveland 14–10
Pittsburgh 34–7
New Orleans 26–6
San Diego 17–14
Houston 30–20
Boston 45–7

Season: 8–6
Points scored: Bengals 312,
  opponents 255
Playoff: Baltimore 17,
  Cincinnati 0

1971: Cincinnati Bengals (NFL)

Philadelphia 37–14
Pittsburgh 10–21
Green Bay 17–20
Miami 13–23
Cleveland 24–27
Oakland 27–31
Houston 6–10
Atlanta 6–9
Denver 24–10
Houston 28–13
San Diego 31–0
Cleveland 27–31
Pittsburgh 13–21
New York Jets 21–35

Season: 4–10
Points scored: Bengals 284,
  opponents 265

1972: Cincinnati Bengals (NFL)

New England 31–7
Pittsburgh 15–10
Cleveland 6–27
Denver 21–10

Kansas City 23–16
Los Angeles 12–15
Houston 30–7
Pittsburgh 17–40
Oakland 14–20
Baltimore 19–20
Chicago 13–3
New York Giants 13–10
Cleveland 24–27
Houston 61–17

Season: 8–6
Points scored: Bengals 299,
  opponents 229

1973: Cincinnati Bengals (NFL)

Denver 10–28
Houston 24–10
San Diego 20–13
Cleveland 10–17
Pittsburgh 19–7
Kansas City 14–6
Pittsburgh 13–20
Dallas 10–38
Buffalo 16–13
New York Jets 20–14
St. Louis 42–24
Minnesota 27–0
Cleveland 34–17
Houston 27–24

Season: 10–4
Points scored: Bengals 286,
  opponents 231
Playoff: Miami 34,
  Cincinnati 16

1974: Cincinnati Bengals (NFL)

Cleveland 33–7
San Diego 17–20
San Francisco 21–3

Washington 28–17
Cleveland 34–24
Oakland 27–30
Houston 21–34
Baltimore 24–14
Pittsburgh 17–10
Houston 3–20
Kansas City 33–6
Miami 3–24
Detroit 19–23
Pittsburgh 3–27

Season: 7–7
Points scored: Bengals 283,
  opponents 259

1975: Cincinnati Bengals (NFL)

Cleveland 24–17
New Orleans 21–0
Houston 21–19
New England 27–10
Oakland 14–10
Atlanta 21–14
Pittsburgh 24–30
Denver 17–16
Buffalo 33–24
Cleveland 23–35
Houston 23–19
Philadelphia 31–0
Pittsburgh 14–35
San Diego 47–17

Season: 11–3
Points scored: Bengals 340,
  opponents 246
Playoff: Oakland 31,
  Cincinnati 28

INDEX